THE MATHESON TRUST

The principal objective of The Matheson Trust is to promote the study of comparative religion from the point of view of the underlying harmony of the great religious and philosophical traditions of the world. This objective is being pursued through such means as audio-visual media, the support and sponsorship of lecture series and conferences, the creation of a website, collaboration with film production companies and publishing companies as well as the Trust's own series of publications.

THE QUEEN AND THE AVATAR

The Queen and the Avatar

Dominique Wohlschlag

translated from the French by
Deborah Bell

THE MATHESON TRUST
For the Study of Comparative Religion

Originally published as
La Reine et l'avatar: mythologie de Krishna,
by Infolio Éditions, Gollion, Switzerland, 2013.

This first English edition published by
The Matheson Trust
PO Box 336
56 Gloucester Road
London SW7 4UB, UK
www.themathesontrust.org

ISBN: 978 1 908092 16 8

British Library Cataloguing-in-Publication Data.
A catalogue record for this book is
available from the British Library.

Typeset by the publishers in Baskerville 10 Pro.

Cover: Rādhā and Kṛṣṇa receiving homage.
Detail from an 18th century Indian manuscript.
Philadelphia Museum of Art
(125th Anniversary Acquisition)
Alvin O. Bellak Collection, 2004-149-71.
Cover design by Susana Marín.

Contents

Preface

In traditional Christian art there is an image of a little naked boy playing with a shell on a beach beside the sea. It is Saint Augustine who is thus portrayed, because he recognised that he was as incapable of exhausting the mystery of the Holy Trinity in his commentaries as the child he had seen on the seashore was unable to bail out the sea in his tiny container. We would like this image to be applied to the present writer, if only because we have never sought to be exhaustive or even systematic. Although we do not abandon what is called 'academic rigour', it is not our goal to place a new stone in the edifice of Oriental scholarship. Rather, our intention is more personal. It arises from a fascination with the figure of Kṛṣṇa as it appears in the *Mahābhārata, Harivaṃśa* and *Bhāgavata-purāṇa*. What really is an avatar? What is the meaning of his often strange or disturbing behaviour? What does his being *incognito* mean, if even partially so? How can he be a joker, transgressor, cunning plotter or seducer? How does he become the founder of a new religion, or the reviver of an old one? These questions have guided our approach and, starting from this perspective, we feel that the speech of thanksgiving that Queen Kuntī addresses to her nephew Kṛṣṇa at the end of the war provides an invaluable clue. Thus, following her speech verse by verse, as it is related in the *Bhāgavata-purāṇa*, we have sought the answers to our questions first in the Indian tradition and then in other religious or philosophical worlds, and finally in our own understanding. If the reader, in following our method, can glean some keys to enrich his own understanding, or simply to revive his interest in this fertile and remarkably homogeneous field of the Indian epic, we will consider ourselves amply rewarded for our efforts.

A note on the transcription of Sanskrit terms

Sanskrit vowels are pronounced very much like Italian vowels, with the exception of the short *a*, which is pronounced like the *u* in the English word 'but'; the long *ā* is pronounced like the *a* in 'father'.

As for the consonants, a reasonable approximation will be obtained by pronouncing *c* as in 'church', *j* as in 'jungle', *ṣ* as in 'shun', *s* as in 'sun', *ś* as something halfway between the other two s's.

The aspirated consonants should be pronounced distinctly; *bh* as in 'cab-horse', *dh* as in 'mad-house', *gh* as in 'dog-house', *ph* as in 'top-hat', and *th* as in 'goat-herd'.

ṛ is a vowel, pronounced midway between *ri* as in 'rivet' and *er* as in 'father'.

[From: Wendy Doniger O'Flaherty, *Hindu Myths*, Penguin Books, 1975.]

N.B.: the proper names of places and personalities of modern India are given in their usual form without diacritical marks.

Introduction

A famous verse from the *Mahābhārata* declares: 'Regarding the goals of man, namely conformity to order (*dharma*), material wealth (*artha*), love (*kāma*) and deliverance (*mokṣa*), everything which is in this text can also be found elsewhere. What is not here cannot be found anywhere else' (1, 62, 53). The all-embracing dimension of the epic, connecting human experience to the unicity of being, seems to be a general feature of all works of this kind which have played a leading role in the genesis of the great civilizations. Their universal value, even if not always explicitly documented, has undoubtedly been a certainty for all their traditional commentators, as well as for the majority of those whose imagination they have fed over the course of time. Moreover, the strength of this fundamental belief can be attested to in the systematic use of these texts, first by philosophers (in the original meaning of the term 'lover of wisdom'), and, secondly, by the saints or traditional interpreters, who have consistently used them as a source and drawn countless illustrations from them in the course of their teachings. We are thinking here of both the *Mahābhārata* and the *Rāmāyaṇa* in India, as well as the *Iliad* and the *Odyssey* or the *Aeneid* in Europe, and of course, above all, of the Bible, for, to the extent it conveys a sacred history, it belongs to this genre. So it is no coincidence if all of the literary classics that we have just mentioned were used, at least at certain times and places, as the basis for the practice of a form of divination which consisted in opening the book at random at any page in order to find a binding response within it to a personal question that had been previously asked.[1] In other words, it was recognized that these synthetic accounts had an oracular value akin to a revelation of supra-human origin, notwithstanding the fact that it was considered that there were degrees in the level of inspiration of these texts. Vedic literature is qualified in India as *śruti* (literally: hearing), meaning that its authors, the *ṛṣi*, were directly responsive to the speech of God which they passed on without alteration. As for the *Mahābhārata* and *Rāmāyaṇa*, they belong to the *smṛti* (literally: memory, reflection), a category of works considered as having a status lower than the previous one, without being considered devoid of inspiration nonetheless, or of a higher intuition.

In fact, the most obvious feature that all epics have in common is without doubt the number of characters of all shapes and sizes who are placed one way or another in many different, often conflicting or dramatic situations, which provide their audience, who can always refer to them analogically, with numerous examples of what behaviour to follow or not. We also know that these heroes, good or evil—but the reality often lies somewhere

---

1 This universal practice extends from such works as the Sibylline books of ancient Rome, to the Qur'ān or again *mutatis mutandis*, to the *I Ching* in the Chinese tradition. But here we leave the domain of the epic properly so called.

in between—are usually called by a number of names which sometimes bewilders the uninitiated on a first reading. The epic style may show in this a concern for not wanting to weary the reader with tedious repetition but, above all, this plurality is primarily a way of transmitting the complexity of a character, if not psychologically, then at least functionally and symbolically, in a context that extends far beyond that of an ordinary novel. Regarding the main figures of these texts, which in India are the *avatāra*,[2] the countless epithets which describe them fulfil a role which is both theological and initiatic. This is eminently the case with the lists of a thousand names given to Viṣṇu or to the goddess (Lalitā) that the devotee may recite one after the other in his spiritual practice,[3] unless he prefers, as is more common, to select one of these names to apply to the Divinity itself through His incarnation.[4]

---

2 The *avatāra* are literally descents (of the divinity amongst men). As Madeleine Biardeau has stressed (2002: 2, 728), the occurrence of this word comes after the appearance of the *Mahābhārata* which only uses the verb *ava-TṚ*, to descend.

3 In the same way Muslims recite the 99 divine names and some Christians recite litanies to the Virgin.

4 Some Orientalists refuse to use the word 'incarnation' in this context, because of the meaning that it has taken on in Christianity, where it is given an exclusive value, related to the historicity of Christ. The latter case appears to be unique in the sacred history of the biblical world and Christians can scarcely admit that a mythological character can 'become flesh'. Theology therefore assigns specific characteristics to the Incarnation of Christ which we seek in vain to find the equivalent of in India. Having said this, however, we shall retain 'incarnation' for *avatāra*, like many other writers, with

Regarding the *Mahābhārata*, we will begin with this observation: as the full *avatāra* of the god Viṣṇu who, in the view of the devotional perspective which primarily interests us here, represents the supreme Principle, Kṛṣṇa stands out as the central figure of the epic. The Hindu who reads and meditates on the divine acts of this character will therefore make this fundamental identity of the hero with the omnipotent deity the master key to the whole work, and consequently any sociological or historical interpretation, for example, will become superficial, or even useless to him. However, other protagonists in the story appear to have quite different degrees of awareness of the avataric nature of Kṛṣṇa. Thus, 'Fools do not recognize me in this human body. They ignore my supreme essence as Lord of creatures,' says Kṛṣṇa to Arjuna. And: 'Only the wise (*mahātman*) attached to the divine nature (*daivī prakṛti*) worship me single-mindedly, recognizing me as the eternal principle of creatures' (*Bhagavad-gītā*, 9, 11 and 13). Similarly, in the *Rāmāyaṇa*, only twelve people, it is said, are aware of the reality of Rāma's avataric nature (Herbert [1949] 1972: 344). This situation is in fact the same as in the Gospel which describes how the person of Christ is perceived by his contemporaries

---

the idea that the analogy with Christianity is in this case more important than the difference. In fact, we are following on this point the Hindus themselves, who do not hesitate to describe Christ as an avatar in order to emphasize the doctrinal relationship. Thus Rāmakṛṣṇa says: 'The avatar is always the same. The one God immersed in the ocean of life incarnates, and is called Krishna. Another time, He plunges, and reemerges somewhere else among mankind and is called Jesus' (Herbert [1949] 1972: 340).

in very different ways. While some fiercely deny his divinity, or at least his authority, even so far as to seek his death at all costs, others do have a certain presentiment of it. The Apostles themselves only gradually discover the true greatness of their master. Thus Thomas has to put his finger in the wounds of the risen Christ in order to recognize Him for who He is. The Indian epic is just as rich in confrontations of this kind, if not more so, given the magnitude of the story. Kaṃsa, the king usurper, slayer of the six older brothers of Balarāma and Kṛṣṇa, does not realize that the latter is none other than the god Viṣṇu, until he ultimately receives from him the blow of the mace which causes his death. This perfect recognition, *in extremis*, besides granting him a complete remission of his sins, assures him instant deliverance. In this respect he is comparable to Pharaoh in the Muslim tradition, who is saved in a similar manner when the waters of the Red Sea close over him after the passage of the Hebrews: 'Pharaoh who was about to be engulfed said, "Yes, I believe: there is only one God in whom the sons of Israel believe, I am among those submitted to Him." God said ... today we will save you in your body that thou mayest be a sign for those who come after you' (Qur'ān 10:90–92, trans. Pickthall).[5] In the same order of ideas, mention may also be made of the good thief, who at the point of death obtained complete remission

5 Such at least is the opinion of Ibn ʿArabī, who declares in the *Fuṣūṣ al-Ḥikam*, 'the general belief in the damnation of Pharaoh is not based on any sacred text' (1975:114). On this point he comes up against the majority of exegetes, who interpret another passage of the Qur'ān (11:96–99) differently, and thus seem to condemn Pharaoh to the same fate of his people.

of his sins, on confessing the divinity of Jesus, crucified beside him (cf. Luke 23: 39–43).

But if the case of Kaṃsa, described as the earthly manifestation of a demon, seems to obey a certain logic, one can legitimately wonder at the doubts or bias of the main heroes who play a vital role in the epic. The *Mahābhārata*, indeed, tells us that they are the great gods of Vedic mythology, who are made to contribute in various ways to this universal drama. One realizes, therefore, quite early on in the story that, as is also the case in the *Iliad*, the gods are forced to take sides in the human conflict, sometimes apparently even 'against their better judgement'. Their obedience to the incarnation of the supreme god is neither automatic, since they are sometimes opposed to him in the war, nor are they always fully aware of who he is when they fight at his side. Among those who fight on the Kaurava rebel clan's side, and so against Kṛṣṇa, it should be noted, are principally Bhīṣma, Vidura and Droṇa, who represent respectively Dyu (Heaven), Dharma (the Cosmic Order) and Bṛhaspati (the Priest of the gods). Their irrevocable allegiance to king Dhṛtarāṣṭra forces them to take his side, despite their affection for their relatives and friends of the other clan. As for Karṇa, the son of Sūrya (the Sun), he represents a different possibility, since he assumes his bellicose commitment voluntarily out of loyalty to Duryodhana and in a spirit of revenge with regard to Arjuna.

But the most striking example of the hesitation of a hero to espouse the cause of the major avatar is given by Arjuna himself. This son of the god Indra has to wait for the episode of the *Bhagavad-gītā*, on the eve of battle, before he really understands who Kṛṣṇa, his faithful companion who serves as his charioteer, is. At the point when Arjuna gives in to utter despair at the thought of having to fight against the members of his own family, the avatar, in a kind of transfiguration, suddenly appears to him in his cosmic form encompassing all the worlds, in order to remove his last doubts and urge him on to fight. Thus, on the side protected by Kṛṣṇa—the clan of the Pāṇḍava—, are, apart from Arjuna himself, Yudhiṣṭhira, the son of Dharma, Bhīma, the son of Vāyu (the Wind) and Dhṛṣtadyumna, the son of Agni (Fire), to name only the most important.[6] The presence of a character that embodies *dharma* in both camps, namely Yudhiṣṭhira on the one side and Vidura on the other, shows that the conflict goes beyond a simple confrontation between 'good and evil' cousins, as some commentators have described the two parties. And when, after the war, Vidura dies, his soul leaves his body and miraculously enters that of his nephew Yudhiṣṭhira, as if to indicate that *dharma* transcends the conflict. Furthermore, the presence of multiple gods divided between the two clans shows that the avataric function cannot be reduced only to the person of Kṛṣṇa, but that it is shared somehow among all the main protagonists in the drama.

Before proceeding further in these analyses, we must make it clear that one encounters, above all in the writing of the *Mahābhārata*, the most explicit expression of a

---

6 In the first volume of *Mythe et épopée*, Dumézil (1986) treats all these equivalences in a very complete fashion. Despite his desire to bring everything back to the ideology of the three functions which is his hobby horse, his analysis is relevant and useful to the understanding of the epic.

fundamental shift that had taken place in the Indian tradition in the centuries before the Christian era.[7] The *sanātana-dharma* (perennial religion, or perennial order) as the Hindus refer to their own tradition, underwent at that time a considerable change in orientation within the spiritual cosmos of India. The disruption of values that accompanied this shift seems to have been 'in tune with the times', to the extent that it marked a sharp reaction against Buddhism and aimed to correct a Brahmanism grown too elitist. Thus it led to what first the Muslims, and then the West, would call Hinduism. But in the Indian consciousness it responded primarily to the passage from the third to the fourth age in the history of humanity, from the *dvāpara-yuga* to the *kali-yuga*, with all the constraints imposed by such a cyclic shift. We are now in the Vaishnavite climate with the emergence of *bhakti* (sharing, love, devotion) that characterizes it. Therefore the path of devotion, *bhakti-yoga*, as defined by Kṛṣṇa in the *Bhagavad-gītā*, is, in this new perspective, placed above the spiritual ways that were predominant in the Vedic period, namely that of

---

[7] Despite their incongruity in the dating of Indian events, the references to the Christian calendar are unavoidable: on the one hand they are convenient for Western readers, and on the other hand they are necessary because of the absence of any uniform Indian calendar. Concerning the date of the writing of the *Mahābhārata*, the least one can say is that the issue is fluid and complex. For example, the *Encyclopedia Universalis* places it between 4 BC and 4 AD! Another problem to resolve is knowing if the writing was by one person (which Madeleine Biardeau, amongst others, believes), or if it was a question of being a work in progress over centuries. While these questions are not without interest, they are outside the scope of the present work.

karman (sacrifice) and *jñāna* (knowledge), without going so far as to invalidate them. The path of *bhakti* is more favourable, however, for the majority, because, as the avatar explains, it is clearly easier than the others. This is the reason why it is better suited to the formidable conditions that would henceforth subjugate mankind, victims of the malice of time, plunged deep in the age of darkness. We will have further opportunity to consider these ideas, but will note in passing that it is in the *Mahābhārata* where the term *bhakti* first appears, if not also the particular spiritual path it designates.

The Vedic pantheon is, therefore, presented in a new perspective, with the presence of a Supreme God to whom all the other ancient deities are subordinate, which some have termed henotheism (*heno* = one), a term that has the advantage of reserving monotheism to the Abrahamic religions. However the Vedic heritage is not denied either. In the *Bhagavad-gītā*, Kṛṣṇa states in this regard: 'It is I who should be known through all the *Veda*. I am the author of the *Vedānta* and the knower of the *Veda*' (15, 15). One can certainly see a parallel here with Christ when he says that he came not to abolish the Scriptures, but to fulfil them (Matthew 5:17–18). Thus, in the Indian context, the *Veda* continue to enjoy an unequalled prestige. But while they were once largely confined to the Brahmin caste and therefore relatively inaccessible to other members of society, they now fade into the background in contrast to a belief which is open to all, with its spirit of redefining the *dharma* by explicitly responding to the emergence of a new need, a new human requirement. The *Veda* appear then as the testimony of a bygone spiritual world upon which we can always draw and that are perpetuated in certain rituals and among certain circles, but in the consciousness and practice of the majority of the faithful they are overshadowed by the more recent religion, which sets aside certain gods and redefines the function of others.

The birth of a prolific and varied mythology, which we are already familiar with in Greece, thus emerges in India as both the cause and consequence of the popularisation of the Brahmanic religion, without it seeming necessary to solve this variant of the paradox of the chicken and the egg. There took place, in a relatively short time, an opening up of the priestly tradition to all kinds of popular currents, together with *ādivāsī*, Dravidian, and even foreign, notably Greek, influences.[8] To understand this evolution fully, it has to be appreciated that originally the Vedic gods only had a theological dimension, in that although they had a clearly defined function, they had a vague personality, 'without any history'. Certainly, as Ananda Coomaraswamy has shown in his well-known *Hinduism and Buddhism*, the *Ṛg-veda* depicts some basic myths such as the killing of the dragon Vṛtra by Indra or the voluntary dismemberment of Puruṣa, the Cosmic Man, in the creation of the world and the establishing of the sacrifice. But we cannot yet speak of a mythology in the usual sense, i.e. a collection of myths describing in narrative mode the actions and deeds of a given pan-

---

[8] The *ādivāsī* are the aborigines of India. The English in their censuses called them the scheduled tribes. They make up about 8 per cent of the population of present day India and are not Hindus at all. As for what the Greeks brought, this dates back to the arrival of Alexander in 4 BC. Some scholars see an influence of the works of Homer in the plot of the *Mahābhārata*.

theon. At the Vedic stage, this figurative language was just beginning. It is important to understand here the multiple consequences of such a shift. The gods represented in the epic met the need for wonderment of the majority, dissatisfied as they were by the dryness of the Vedic rites and the elliptical nature of the hymns that accompanied them, whatever their extraordinary poetic value. In addition, the colourful unfolding of their actions, which made the gods more concrete and even strangely human in their incarnations by representing them through an explicit iconography, giving them attributes, and depicting them with all their alliances and conflicts, went hand in hand with a considerable flourishing of the arts that were nourished by this manna. First came literature, then theatre, sculpture, dance, painting and many more, and lastly, let us not forget, architecture; for the gods had come down to earth and made it sacred in a new way. They lived their adventures in specific locations that pilgrims still hasten to visit and, as they took on a visible form, the arts were legitimately able to represent them in a thousand different ways. Finally, the statues, which represented them and were considered 'living' after their rite of consecration, needed a home to inhabit, and this gave rise to the art of temple building. While the Vedic sacrifice was performed outdoors in a sacred space, specifically in nature itself, which was like a sanctuary, it was Hinduism, that is *bhakti*, that created the temple. Thus the great religious architectural achievements of India appeared almost immediately after the dissemination of the epic, from the fourth century AD, and therefore the rite of *pūjā* (devotional worship) replaced *yajña* (sacrifice itself). This impact of religion on the various art forms was not without importance in its social consequences, as it presented the craftsmen with great challenges, and gave them, *de facto*, an undisputedly important status, inspiring the development of a multitude of skills formerly reserved for castes which had certainly been less valued. The flowering of the arts, crafts and techniques[9] which followed was a sign of the times. It offered *homo faber* new initiatory ways, new supports for meditation, linked to the archetypes inherent in the processing and fashioning of the material, which would remain spiritually effective as long as this symbolic dimension persisted in the minds of men and the industrial world did not come to ruin everything with its immoderate thirst for productivity. Chapter 35 of Exodus describes at length a comparable cyclical phenomenon, when Moses invites all those qualified among his people to mobilize to build the Tabernacle, the dwelling of Yahweh: 'Them hath He filled with wisdom of heart, to work all manner of work, of the engraver, and of the cunning workman, and of the embroiderer, in blue, and in purple, in scarlet, and in fine linen, and of the weaver, even of them that do any work, and of those that devise cunning work. Then wrought Bezaleel and Aholiab, and every wise hearted man, in whom the Lord put wisdom and understanding, to know how to work all manner of work for the service of the Sanctuary, according to all that the Lord had commanded' (Exodus 35:35–36:1, KJV).

---

9 The words *ars* in Latin and *technē* in Greek cover the three meanings in one word. It is worth remembering also the primary meaning of *sophia*, wisdom, which means technical skill.

In the West it may be supposed that Greek mythology was born of a similar movement, but we lack sufficient evidence from pre-Homeric times to document such a development, in the way we can in India. With Rome, in contrast, it was only relatively late, under Greek influence, that a mythology was imported in the second century BC. Consequently, the ancient Roman religion preserved more than one trait in common with the Vedic religion, a fact that has been eloquently attested to by Georges Dumézil. Be that as it may, it is still important to note this: the development of mythology is ultimately perceived by the Hindus as being both a sign of progress and degeneration. It was a form of progress in the sense that, in breaking, at least to some extent, the barriers of caste, which were too sclerotic, the *dharma* found a new vitality that it had lost.[10] With the epic, India settled old scores, first with a Brahmanism that was too elitist, and, secondly with Buddhism, not by denying the latter outright, but by including it, so to speak, in a broader context. This kind of *Reconquista* would be the prelude to the almost total disappearance of this religion in India. Finally, the birth of the epic marks, in the Hindu collective imagination at least, a degeneration in that it appears as a sign of decadence inherent in the course of time, as described by the doctrine of the four ages, since it inaugurated the troubled times in which we now live. The man of the Vedic period, who belonged to the *dvāpara-yuga*, the Indian equivalent of the Bronze Age of the Greek tradition, had a perception of the sacred which

---

10 Inversely, with the coming of the Muslims to India in the 12–13th centuries, the caste system became rigid as a sort of identity reflex.

was more immediate, more intuitive, and more intimate. Performing sacrifices outdoors in a consecrated space, without the need for any divine representations, he had the entire cosmos as his temple and so communicated more directly with heaven.[11] Now, in the *kali-yuga*, the Iron Age of the Greek tradition, the devotee cannot live without tangible supports; he needs images to express his faith and a more explicit spiritual guidance.

Any new law, be it divine or human, necessarily corrects a fall by offering ways to mitigate its effects, but this is justifiable only because the excesses, which were accidental, have now become the norm. In this sense, each redrawing of the *dharma* inevitably confirms a more degraded state,[12] although for humanity it appears, *a priori*, that suddenly valuable opportunities have opened up. However, the balance is actually more fragile. In the first age *dharma* is compared to a bull that stands firmly on four legs. But with each passage from one age to another he loses a leg, until in the present age, he teeters very precariously on one. This understanding of the changing world is certainly at the very antipodes of

---

[11] The word *templum* in archaic Latin describes precisely a part of the sky where the diviner can particularly observe the flight of birds. It was only later that it came to be applied to a solid construction. In the Imperial era, Tacitus noticed with admiration that the Germans, who did not have temples, thought it sacrilegious to enclose the gods between four walls.

[12] Unlike the Hindus who are deeply attached to their mythic past, Christians do not cherish a particular nostalgia for the time before Christ's coming and the ensuing era of Grace. The Muslims in contrast see Islam as the restoration of the religion of Abraham, the *ḥanīf*, whose practice was pure and orthodox.

the beliefs of those who see in the systematic recognition of various rights or in the enactment of new laws the supposed progress of humanity.

1

The Heroes of the *Mahābhārata*

We said earlier that the central figure of the *Mahābhārata* was Kṛṣṇa, which is certainly the case.[1] But given the fact that he only appears late in the events of the story, a number of other protagonists in the narrative can be taken as playing the lead role each in their turn. From a strictly literary perspective, this Indian epic is remarkable in that the different characters summarize within themselves, according to the point of view one adopts, the essential meaning of the entire plot. We are

[1] We have provided in an appendix a brief summary of the main episodes of the epic which are necessary to the understanding of our analysis. The reader unfamiliar with the *Mahābhārata* is encouraged to read these few pages before going further. See abridged versions in English by Kamala Subramanian, Ramesh Menon, William Buck, R. K. Narayan, Romesh C. Dutt, John D. Smith, and a complete version by Ganguli Kisari Mohan and Gupta Neteesh. Also we will take advantage of this note to say that when we speak of the (Krishnaite) epic we also include in this term, in addition to the *Mahābhārata*, the other two works that are essential to it, that is the *Harivaṃśa* and the *Bhāgavata-purāṇa*. More explicit reference to the latter will be made further below.

dealing with a kind of jigsaw puzzle in which no part is superfluous. Thus Vyāsa, who passes for the traditional author of this enormous work, shows the demiurgic grip he has on it by giving himself the role of 'biological' father to the two brothers who are the source of the dynastic struggle, namely the blind Dhṛtarāṣṭra and the bloodless Pāṇḍu, as well as their wise younger brother Vidura. He therefore is not merely a privileged witness of the events who narrates what he has seen, but far more than that he manifests in a unique way the fact that he eminently carries within himself the contents of the story that he transmits to posterity. World literature offers few examples so successful as this close identification between the author of a work and one of its key actors.

To the extent that it is Yudhiṣṭhira, the eldest Pāṇḍava, who is called upon to be the king of Bhārata, it is then he who plays the central role in this drama. The importance of his function in the warrior world of the *kṣatriya* emerges, above all, from the fact that most of the teachings given by the various sages which occur in the course of the story are directly addressed to him. His slow psychological and spiritual development, as well as the authority he exerts over his brothers, consequently greatly determines the general unfolding of events in the epic.

Arjuna, for his part, can also claim the limelight as the flawless and invincible hero with whom the reader instinctively identifies. From the perspective of *bhakti*, he embodies the perfect devotee, as shown, among other things, by the representation on his banner of Hanumān, the general of the army of monkeys, who with unfailing dedication served Rāma, the previous incarnation of

Viṣṇu at the end of the second age.[2] The importance of Arjuna is also apparent from the fact that it is to him that Kṛṣṇa explicitly addresses his teaching in the famous episode of the *Bhagavad-gītā*, whose relatively short text is found in full in Book 6 of the *Mahābhārata*. Even if most indologists believe that this philosophical dialogue is a later addition, the doctrinal coherence of this passage with respect to the whole work is so perfect, that it is no exaggeration to say that it expresses its quintessence.

Draupadī, the wife in common of the five Pāṇḍava brothers, in turn occupies a central role as she herself embodies the cause of the war, when after Duryodhana has just won her at dice, he asks his brother Duḥśāsana to strip her in the middle of the assembly in order to humiliate his cousins. Although born of the sacrificial Fire, she personifies, in this case, rather the Earth, which Duryodhana wants to possess in order to exercise his despotic power. This passage is undoubtedly the most dramatic episode in the entire epic. It lies at the climax of the plot development and, like the crucifixion in the Gospel, it marks the extreme low point in the tragedy of the Pāṇḍava, when all seems lost, when *dharma* seems to have been completely rejected in this lower world. Then, at this critical moment, Draupadī has the presence of mind to invoke Kṛṣṇa inwardly, although he is not

---

2 Although the *Rāmāyaṇa* tells a story situated in a period mythologically previous to the *Mahābhārata*, it is not certain if it was written earlier than the latter. In fact, the *Mahābhārata* tells incidentally, in brief outline, the whole plot of the *Rāmāyaṇa*. Does this mean that it summarizes an existing work, or that this second epic constitutes a development of that episode? The question remains open for indologists to solve.

physically present at this terrible scene. By the power of his *māyā*, in answer to her prayer, he makes his protégé's sari limitless, thus ridiculing Duḥśāsana who is unable to unravel it to its end. In this way he preserves the purity of the young woman and allows the Pāṇḍava to obtain, at the same time, a reprieve for a while.[3] In the traditional approach that consists of understanding the epic as an inward drama in which the five husbands and their wife are seen as an allegory of the five senses and the *manas*, the inner faculty which receives the perceptions, it is man as such that the avatar saves in the end from the extreme pride of the ego, represented by Duryodhana. This reprieve, however, is only temporary or virtual, since it requires from the Pāṇḍava a further series of purificatory and initiatory tests.

We could also see in this vain attempt to strip the heroine, who is entirely abandoned to the grace of Kṛṣṇa, an image of modern science which greedily attempts to penetrate the secrets of nature, but is constantly confronted by a new layer, a new veil. The nakedness of Nature is thus reserved for her legitimate husbands, who then represent the traditional sciences. This interpretation is also supported by the god Brahmā who, in addressing Kṛṣṇa, says: 'The scholars can count over time the grains of dust of the earth, the water droplets of fog and the stars of heaven. But who can measure your qualities, you who came to earth for the good of all, and are the very es-

---

[3] One finds the same expression of an immediate deliverance from evil attacks thanks to the invocation of the divinity in several episodes of Christian hagiography. For example, Saint Agnes, on being undressed by her executioners, sees, in answer to her prayer, her hair suddenly grow to hide her nakedness.

sence (*ātman*) of these qualities?' (*Bhāgavata-purāṇa*, 10, 14, 7). Finally, let us note that, as with Helen in the Trojan War, it is also a woman in the Indian epic that ultimately the warring parties fight over. We will return later to this key episode of the epic.

The arrogant and ambitious Duryodhana can also be considered a major character; without his endless thirst for power, without his relentless determination to destroy the Pāṇḍava, the *Mahābhārata* would lose all dramatic effect and the war would never have happened. But 'it must needs be that scandals come,' and we learn in the course of the story that he actually embodies the *kali-yuga*, the age of the lowest throw of the dice, when you can only score a one (*kali*).[4] It little signifies whether we count the beginning of the dark period from the day of Duryodhana's birth, or as some do, eager to place the entire life of Kṛṣṇa in the third age, from the year of Kṛṣṇa's death, thirty-six years after the end of the war. This second opinion seems less pertinent, though, if one considers that the avatar explicitly addresses his message to men already affected by this change in cyclical conditions.

If the *Mahābhārata*, as a universal conflict which throws the world into chaos by redistributing the cards (to use another image), contains strange analogies to the Second World War, then we cannot fail to compare the insatiable Duryodhana, who is full of hatred, to Hitler,

---

4 Dice in India have a rectangular shape with only four numbered sides. These numbers correspond to the mythological ages, the *yuga*, which have a decreasing length in the ratio of: 4, 3, 2, 1, the 1 having in this context the lowest value, corresponding to the final period of the cycle.

who in historical fashion concentrated in himself all the horror of the conflict.[5] It may be noted with regard to this that the mythographer and the historian have at least one goal in common, that of 'keeping memories (*smṛti*) alive for posterity' in order to try to teach men a lesson. The difference is that the first mentioned role is situated in a sort of ontological verticality, whereas the second is situated in a chronological horizontality. In any case, in the Western tradition history has occupied, since the time of Herodotus, an especially prestigious role that has profoundly influenced Christianity; for indeed, many Christians regard Jesus as a divine manifestation infinitely greater than any that the ancient pantheons were able to produce by the very fact that he is a historical figure, and this notwithstanding that the Christ they worship obviously transcends history.[6] This divergence

---

[5] A global—that is to say universal—conflict, cannot be interpreted in the Hindu context except as the passage in a downward direction to a new cyclical era. The world could not be the same before and after such an upheaval. In addition, despite the principle of self-defence, one cannot claim that between the warring 'cousins' there is just one good clan and one evil one, as we have said above. They are caught, despite themselves, in a storm that exceeds them. Moreover, the author of the epic shows a singular intuition when he speaks of the disastrous effects of the Kurukṣetra war on nature in general. The heroes have at their disposition weapons of 'mass destruction' which they are reluctant to use for this reason. 'Even the grass trembles' at the possible implementation of such a means of annihilation. This environmental awareness is the more remarkable when one considers that at the time of writing of these texts, men fought with bows and swords, and no one could imagine, for example, the devastating results of an atomic bomb.

[6] On the Indian concept of history, see below the commentary

of views is linked to the differences inherent in the conceptions of time that varying civilizations develop. We will return later to this important point.

The list of the most significant players in this story of Vyāsa's could easily be extended, as the epic contains other characters who play, at one time or another, a key role in the unfolding of the myth. This construction highlights the complexity of an exceptionally ingenious 'scenario', which, as we have seen, gives the renaissance of the *sanātana-dharma* a new organic coherence on the basis of a structural rereading, a kind of *aggiornamento* or updating of the Vedic religion.[7] But it is time now to introduce the character who is the subject of this book, namely Queen Kuntī.

---

on verse 11. Having said this, a specialist on the question of the historic Jesus informed us that today researchers who deny the concrete existence of Jesus have become extremely rare. Five things seem accepted according to his own words: that he lived in Palestine under Pontius Pilate, that he was baptised, that he had disciples, that he talked of the Kingdom of Heaven and that he was condemned to death. A little, no doubt, but it is also a great deal.

[7] It is also interesting to note that if Vaishnavism was constructed *a priori* on the basis of the literary genre of the epic (*itihāsa*), the Śaivite and Śaktic mythologies, in contrast, were developed in the corpus of the *Purāṇa* (cf. ch. 3), and thus later.

2

The Role of Kuntī

Kuntī is Kṛṣṇa's aunt, that is to say, his father Vasudeva's sister, but in order to understand the kinship between the main protagonists in the epic, one must go back to the founding ancestor of the lunar dynasty, namely the god Candra, the Moon.[1] In the early period of this dynasty, King Yayāti had two wives who each bore him a son, Yadu and Pūru. But the king, after a thousand year reign, decided to hand over power only to the son who would give him his youth in exchange. The elder Yadu refused and was therefore disinherited, whereas Pūru accepted this proposal. Yadu became the ancestor of the Yādava, the senior branch of the line, who were condemned to exile, and among whom was born, much later, Śūra, the father of Kuntī and Vasudeva. As to Pūru, he kept the reins of power in the hands of his own offspring, the Paurava, to whom were related at the

---

1 All the planets in the etymological sense of wandering stars (as opposed to the fixed stars), including the sun and the moon, are male gods in India. In contrast, the previous incarnation of Viṣṇu before Kṛṣṇa, namely King Rāma, belongs to the solar dynasty descended from Sūrya, the Sun.

time of the *Mahābhārata* both the Pāṇḍava, who were the sons of Pāṇḍu, and the Kaurava, who were the sons of Dhṛtarāṣṭra, Duryodhana being their leader.[2] Thus Kṛṣṇa is a distant cousin of the members of the two clans who are vying for power. Certainly, there is in this genealogy a bit of 'cheating', if one takes into account the fact that, of the members of the dynasty, Dhṛtarāṣṭra, Pāṇḍu and Vidura on the one hand, are in reality the children of a surrogate father, namely the Brahmin Vyāsa, and on the other hand, that Karṇa and the five Pāṇḍava have divine fathers. But through the principle of adoption, all these characters are truly related to the lunar dynasty and are considered *kṣatriya*, whose code of behaviour they uphold, which is all that really matters here. Such a case is also reminiscent of Jesus, whom Matthew (1:1–16) presents as the son of Abraham, David and Joseph, independently of his directly divine origin.

Kuntī, for her part, was given up for adoption by her father, the Yādava Śūra, to King Kuntibhoja, who had no children. It was from the latter, therefore, that she got her name. In reality, Kunti (with an -i and not -ī) was the name of the people ruled by this king, whose capital was Surāṣṭra, the current Surat in Gujarat. The proper name of this heroine is actually Pṛthā, hence the name of Pṛthā-Kuntī. Pṛthā means 'Flat' like the palm of the hand, which is also a secondary meaning of the word. Since any name has to have a positive meaning, we can assume that it means either a soul without harshness or roughness,

---

2 Actually the Pāṇḍava, as the sons of Pāṇḍu, are also descendants of Kuru, thus they are likewise Kaurava, along with the sons of Dhṛtarāṣṭra. But in practice, the two enemy clans are designated in this way.

or a perfect ability to receive. The same Sanskrit root is found in the most common word for the Earth, Pṛthivī, the Vast Expanse, who is a goddess. Now, the ability to receive was indeed manifested to an eminent degree by the young princess, when she welcomed the Brahmin Durvāsas, the 'Badly-dressed One', at the court of her father. This character crops up throughout the centuries, since he had already appeared previously in connection with the same dynasty at the time of the famous Śakuntalā,[3] to whom he caused problems on the pretext that she had inhospitably received him. He is considered to be a particularly irascible incarnation of Śiva, but when faced with the flawless hospitality of Kuntī, he was obliged to be grateful, and as a reward he gave her a *mantra*, a sacred formula, that allowed her to conceive children from any god whom she invoked. One day, dazzled by the sun (Sūrya) and still incredulous as to the effectiveness of the *mantra*, the princess uttered the formula just 'to try it out'. Immediately the god appeared and she conceived a child, somewhat in spite of herself, while miraculously recovering her virginity *post partum*. In this way she gave birth to a magnificent little boy born with golden earrings and a breastplate. Unfortunately, since she was obliged to conceal her 'guilt', Kuntī was forced to abandon her offspring, whom she placed, like Romulus and Remus, the children of Rhea Silvia begotten by the god Mars, in a basket that

---

3 Śakuntalā is the heroine of Kālīdāsa's drama of the same name, which was translated very early on in France. This is the Sacontale of *La Chanson du mal-aimé* by Apollinaire. Śakuntalā was also depicted in a famous sculpture by Camille Claudel.

she entrusted to the waters of a river.[4] The son of Sūrya was then found by a couple from the low charioteer caste who gave him the name of Karṇa. Now, during a tournament, because of his modest caste, he was scorned by Arjuna who refused to fight against him, not knowing anything, of course, of his true origins. Full of hatred and spite, Karṇa then took the side of the Kaurava, alongside his protector, Duryodhana. It was only after his death in single combat against this same Arjuna, on the tenth day of the war of Kurukṣetra, that in a particularly tragic scene, Kuntī revealed the whole story to the Pāṇḍava, asking them to make the funeral rites for the older brother they had never known. It was then her painful misfortune to have to undergo the reproaches of her five younger sons who berated her bitterly for having hidden the truth. Incidentally, the tragic fate of Karṇa is not without analogy to that of Phaethon, the son of Helios, raised in ignorance of his father, who tried, once the secret of his birth had been revealed, to become the driver of the chariot of the sun as proof of his ancestry. But unable to control it he scorched the earth and was struck down by Zeus, the Greek god nearest in function and mythology to Indra, whom Arjuna embodies precisely in the Indian epic.

We will not recount in detail here Queen Kuntī's whole story, but we should mention that after the birth of Karṇa she married Pāṇḍu, who became king before

[4] Livy, 1. 4. These two myths obviously recall the adventure of Moses, who was also consigned to the waters of a river by his mother, or Sargon of Akkad (3rd millennium BC), the sovereign 'saved from the water'. We can also find similar traits in the legends relating to the birth of Cyrus the Great or Perseus.

his older brother who was blind. However, as Pāṇḍu was the victim of a curse condemning him to death if he had sexual relations with any of his wives, she told her husband the gift that she had been granted, and offered to invoke the gods to give him descendants. Unable to do otherwise, the king agreed on condition that he be the one to choose the begetters of 'his' children. Thus from the gods Dharma, Vāyu and Indra were born respectively the heroes Yudhiṣṭhira, Bhīma and Arjuna. Then, passing her *mantra* on to her co-wife Mādrī, who was jealous of her good fortune, Kuntī allowed her to conceive the twins Nakula and Sahadeva with the aid of the Aśvin gods. Five brothers thus formed the Pāṇḍava clan, united among themselves like the fingers of the palm of the hand and who would be the future co-husbands of the beautiful Draupadī. In Vedic hermeneutics Kuntī and Mādrī appear as incarnations respectively of the two daughters of Dakṣa (Ritual Art), namely Siddhi (Realization) and Dhṛti (Constancy). One should note in passing the presence of mind of Mādrī, who on receiving Kuntī's permission to use the *mantra* once, took the opportunity to invoke the twin gods and obtain two sons in one go! Now, Pāṇḍu, who could no longer resist temptation, ventured one day to unite with Mādrī and died immediately. Madly in love, Mādrī threw herself on the pyre of her husband, and by this spontaneous act inaugurated the practice of *satī* which continues, in a few cases, right up to the present day. Following this event, Kuntī decided to adopt Nakula and Sahadeva formally as her own children, and on some occasions she even said that these last two, especially Nakula who was her favourite, were dearer to her than her own sons.

But we will now pass over the many adventures of the Queen to come to the episode that directly interests us here. At the end of the war, Aśvatthāman, the son of the Brahmin Droṇa (the weapon master and guru of the Pāṇḍava, unfortunately obliged by allegiance to fight against his former disciples), who is one of the three sole survivors of the Kaurava army, decides to avenge his clan by killing all the remnants of the enemy dynasty. First, he manages to kill the five sons of Draupadī, who had been successively begotten by her five husbands, while mistaking them in the dark for their fathers. But that does not satisfy his revenge. Abhimanyu, Arjuna's son by a second marriage to Subhadrā, Kṛṣṇa's sister, who died heroically on the battlefield at the age of sixteen, has left his wife, Princess Uttarā, bearing the last hope of the dynasty, the future Parikṣit.[5] Now, Aśvatthāman, making unlawful use of the *brahmāstra*, a terrible weapon entrusted to him by his father, manages to kill the embryo in Uttarā's womb so that she gives birth to a stillborn child.[6] This is when the women of the palace

[5] Madeleine Biardeau (2002: 2, 481) suggests Uttarā as meaning 'she who makes one go beyond', which works well! But Uttarā means 'the Best', and this identification of the name of the heroine with *uttārā* is based on hermeneutics. As for Parikṣit, named by Kṛṣṇa himself, it has the meaning of 'He who stays' (*ibid.*: 2, 475), but with the idea of all-encompassing, 'He who stays around, encompasses', like the new protector king of *dharma* that he is destined to become.

[6] Aśvatthāman, with his desire for destruction, is an incarnation of Śiva, or at least is possessed by him in his terrible aspect as Rudra. The fact that he is shown in a negative light, with an unfriendly nature and an inability to use his weapons properly, as he shows when he is unable to recall the *brahmāstra* once it

with Queen Kuntī at their head intervene to ask Kṛṣṇa to revive the baby. From the strict point of view of literary drama, this episode may not appear to be very successful. More than any other, it seems 'farfetched'. We would have liked, possibly, the implementation of a more subtle narrative artifice from an author as ingenious as the creator of this epic, so rich in eventful happenings of all kinds, but that's the way it is; it was no doubt necessary that 'the seed must die' before the triumphal recovery of the kingdom of Bhārata. Surprinsingly though, there is another later text which brings a slight alteration to the plot, perhaps with the intention of correcting this 'defect'; this new version thereby introduces the hymn of thanksgiving by Kuntī which will now be the focus of our attention.

---

has been released, or the *cakra* that Kṛṣṇa lends him and which is too heavy for him, indicates that we are in the Vaishnavite world here rather than the Śaivite.

3

The *Bhāgavata-purāṇa*

A variation on the episode concerning the saving of Parikṣit's life is found in the *Bhāgavata-purāṇa* (1, 8, 18–43), which tells us that it was Uttarā, in fact, who rushed to Kṛṣṇa when he was preparing to return home to Dvārakā, and begged him for protection against Aśvatthāman's weapon, which had already been launched and was threatening the embryo in her womb. On seeing the poorly-armed Pāṇḍava ready to defend the young woman at the risk of their lives, Kṛṣṇa brandished his discus to protect them all and destroyed the effects of the missile. He thus saved the last hope of the lunar dynasty by giving its descendants a reprieve to enable them to live through the last age, before its culmination in the final destruction of the cycle. Among those present with the young mother during this event were Draupadī and her five husbands, the Pāṇḍava, as well as Subhadrā, Kṛṣṇa's sister, wife of Arjuna and grandmother of the unborn child, and Kuntī, Kṛṣṇa's aunt and Parikṣit's great-grandmother. In her capacity as the eldest person present, it is she who expresses everybody's feelings in giving thanks to her nephew. As it is these words that we propose to comment on,[1] we are obliged to say something about the work they are drawn from.

The *Bhāgavata-purāṇa* or *Śrīmad-bhāgavata* belongs, as its first name implies, to the literary genre of the *Purāṇa* (the Ancient Scriptures), which form an extremely important corpus of texts in the genesis of Hinduism, and which tradition universally ascribes to the famous Vyāsa (the Diffuser), the designated author of the *Mahābhārata*. In this case, though, it is rather a question of the name of Vyāsa being used because of its prestige, to enhance the importance of the *Purāṇa*. These scriptures are generally dated roughly from the 4th to the 8th centuries BC, a period in any case much later than that estimated for the writing of the two great epics of the *Rāmāyaṇa* and *Mahābhārata*. The *Purāṇa* are traditionally thirty-six in number; eighteen of them are considered major (*mahāpurāṇa*) and eighteen minor (*upapurāṇa*). The principal eighteen are then divided in their turn into three groups of six, according to the three *guṇa*, the fundamental qualities of the created world, to which we will have more occasions to return: *sattva*, the principle of verticality and preservation, *rajas*, the expansive and creative power, and *tamas*, the force of inertia and destruction. The sattvic group (*sāttvika*) is thus attributed to Viṣṇu, the rajasic (*rājasika*) to Brahmā, and the tamasic (*tāmasika*) to Śiva. Of unequal length, the *Purāṇa* are normally written in five sections, dealing respectively with the creation (*sarga*), the re-creation (*prati-*

1 Swami Prabhupāda has also published a commentary on this passage: *The Teachings of Queen Kuntī*. Although our approach is very different from his and not dependent on an exclusivist *bhakti*, we have found it quite useful.

sarga), genealogies of the gods and sages (*vaṃśa*), the history of mankind (*manvantara*), and the genealogy of the kings (*vaṃśānucarita*). Although their overall content is mythological, they also comprise, especially in the last-mentioned section, important elements in relation to the history of ancient India. However, what makes them so popular is the immense collection of legends they contain, and that they communicate spiritual teachings to all, irrespective of caste, thus being far removed from the elitist spirit of the ancient *Veda*, reserved as it was only for Brahmins.

The *Bhāgavata-purāṇa* is therefore connected to the Vaishnavite group. It is considered one of the genre's finest works and is also distinguished by its length, since it contains nearly 18,000 verses (over a thousand pages in translation), divided into twelve books. The Vaishnavites revere it as a sacred text, especially those of them who belong to the Krishnaite sect, which dates back to the saint Caitanya, a 15th century Bengali. In this capacity many passages from this work are recited daily by devotees. There is even a particular ritual practice of reading the entire book in seven days. In relation to the mythology of Kṛṣṇa, the *Bhāgavata-purāṇa* complements the text of the *Mahābhārata* ending with the exploits of the god after the war is finished (in the first book), and telling, as it also does in the *Harivaṃśa*, the first part of his life (from the 10th book onwards). One can only be struck by the extraordinary homogeneity of this immense body of material which takes up the same stories, completing, developing and interpreting them in various ways, but always in accordance with the basic idea. Homeric mythology, with all its prolongations (including the *Aeneid* in

Latin), and the Matter of Britain, with the story of King Arthur and the Grail, awaken in the West a comparable wonderment and have exerted an equally important influence on the arts. But quantitatively, Indian mythology is considerably larger and, more importantly, it inspires, even at the present time, millions, or even hundreds of millions of followers in the most concrete fashion possible. On this scale, all of the sacred history of Christian civilization would have to be added to the contributions of Greece and Britain to obtain a valid equivalent in the West.

4

Kuntī's Hymn of Thanksgiving
(*Bhāgavata-purāṇa*, 1, 8, 18–43)

Kṛṣṇa has just saved the life of the little Parikṣit upon whom all the hopes of the Pāṇḍava depend. On leaving to go home to Dvārakā, he is thanked by Kuntī, who speaks on behalf of all the members of the royal family.

Kuntī said:

1. *I salute the Primordial Man, the Lord who is beyond nature, who is indiscernible, though abiding both within and without all creatures.*

2. (*I salute thee*)[1] *in my ignorance, thou who, covered by the veil of illusion, art Adhokṣaja, the Imperishable, who is hidden from the foolish who do not recognise the dancer in his costume.*

3. *How can we women know thee,* (*who came to earth*) *to teach the path of devotion to the wise and*

[1] The first hemistich of this *śloka* is grammatically the continuation of the previous one.

pure of heart, (destined) for the highest realization (parama-haṃsa)?

4. *Homage to thee, Kṛṣṇa, son of Vasudeva and joy of Devakī, homage to Govinda, the young adopted son of the cowherd Nanda.*

5. *Homage to thee, O lotus-navelled One, homage to thee, who wearest garlands of lotus, homage to thee the lotus-eyed, homage to thee, the soles of whose feet bear the mark of the lotus.*

6. *O Master of the senses, O Omnipresent Lord, just as the long-imprisoned Devakī tormented by the wicked Kaṃsa, was released by thee, have I, with my sons, been released from countless misfortunes thanks to thy protection.*

7. *O Hari, thou hast already saved us from poison, a great fire, a threatening man-eater, a humiliating gathering, the torments of exile in the forest, and then in battle after battle, the countless darts hurled by great warriors, and, finally, Droṇa's son's weapon.*

8. *May these misfortunes be continuously repeated again and again, O Lord of the world. May thy manifestation, O Lord, put an end to the repetition of births.*

9. *The man drunk with arrogance because of his birth, his power, his learning or his beauty is unable*

to submit to thee, who art a pasture for those who have nothing.

10. *I salute Him who is the wealth of those who have nothing, the One whose existence is independent of the fundamental qualities of the world. I salute Him who finds His joy in Himself, Who is peaceful, the Master of the monists.*

11. *I see in thee Time which reigns (over all things), without beginning or end, the Omnipresent, whose relentless onward march makes no distinction anywhere between his creatures, notwithstanding the conflicts that tear them apart.*

12. *O Lord, no one understands thy intentions in thy life here-below. Thou dost deceive men. No one is loved or hated by thee and yet in the minds of men thou dost seem partial.*

13. *O Soul of the universe, thy birth and thy action among the beasts, men, sages and sea monsters is ever a mystery, O thou who art non-born and non-acting.*

14. *When thou didst commit mischief, the milkmaid (Yaśodā) immediately took a rope (to tie thee to a mortar). Thine eyes filled with tears and thy collyrium became smudged. Troubled by apprehension thou didst lower thy head. I was amazed for Fear itself fears thee.*

15. *Some say that thou, the non-born, were born in the lineage of the beloved Yadu to the glory of this man of good reputation (Yudhiṣṭhira?) as sandalwood is to the glory of the mountains of Malaya.*

16. *Others believe that thou didst come into the world in answer to the prayer of Vasudeva and Devakī. Thou art the non-born come to establish peace on earth and kill those who hate the gods.*

17. *Still others believe that thou wert born at the request of Brahmā to alleviate the burden of the world, like a ship sinking due to an excessive load.*

18. *Still others (think thou wert born) so that the hearing, memory and reverence (of and for thy beneficent actions) may come to the aid of those who suffer in this world.*

19. *Men who constantly listen to the story of thine acts, who sing them, who invoke thee, who remember thee, who rejoice in thee, these men contemplating thy lotus feet instantly gain cessation of the cycle of births and deaths.*

20. *Now that thou hast accomplished what thou didst intend to do, O mighty Lord, wilt thou abandon us, we thy friends who live only by thee, we who have no other refuge but thy lotus feet, while the kings of the world plunge us into anxiety?*

21. *What will become of us, we mere individuals, we Pāṇḍava and Yādava, when thou who art the Master of the senses, are no longer visible?*

22. *The earth, O Bearer of the mace, will no longer shine then, as it shines today trodden by thy feet that leave their footprints.*

23. *All these happy people, this luxuriant vegetation, the forests, mountains, rivers, oceans, thrive only thanks to thy glance.*

24. *O Lord of the universe, O Soul of the universe, O Form of the universe, cut this strong bond of affection which binds me to my family, the Pāṇḍava and Vṛṣṇi.*

25. *O Sovereign of Madhu, may my thoughts never have any other object than thee. May they find (in thee) their joy, like the Ganges flowing into the ocean.*

26. *O blessed Lord Kṛṣṇa, O friend of Kṛṣṇa, O Bull of the Vṛṣṇi, O thou who without losing thy strength, destroyeth the dynasties of kings who harm the earth, O Govinda, O thou who dost put an end to the suffering of cows, initiates and gods, O Descent (of God on earth), O Lord of the way, O Master of the universe, O God, homage to thee.*

5

Commentary

Kuntī said:

1. *I salute the Primordial Man, the Lord who is beyond nature, who is indiscernible, though abiding both within and without all creatures.*

Like Thomas who, confronted with Jesus, exclaims, 'My Lord and my God!' the Queen at the outset addresses her nephew in full consciousness of his divinity. He is to her, according to Vedic terminology, the Primordial Man (*puruṣa_ādya*) prior to all creatures.[1] By saying this she identifies her interlocutor with the ancient Puruṣa, the Cosmic Man, who by his fully assumed dismemberment, his gift of self, creates the world and establishes the sacrifice (*Ṛg-veda*, 10.90). At the beginning of song 4 of the *Bhagavad-gītā*, Kṛṣṇa tells Arjuna that he had already, once before, taught the way to Vivasvat, the Sun god, who, in turn, transmitted this knowledge to Manu, the epic 'Adam', the progenitor of the human race. By this strange assertion he provokes the amazement of

[1] The Primordial Man of the Hindu tradition is *al-insān al-qadīm* of Islam and the *Ādam qadmōn* of Judaism.

his companion who, seeing in him only a contemporary, born 'under the sun', asks him for an explanation. In contrast to her son, Kuntī has already realized from the beginning of her hymn of thanksgiving that her nephew is 'the imperishable Self (*ātman*), without beginning, the Lord of all beings,' to use the words of Kṛṣṇa in response to Arjuna.

The principle of anteriority referred to here is actually the same shown by Wisdom, as attested in Proverbs (8: 22): 'The Lord possessed me in the beginning of his way, before his works of old. I was set up from everlasting, from the beginning, or ever the earth was' (KJV). This prerogative is, what is more, common to all prophetic manifestations of the divine Mercy, whether male or female, such as those found in the most diverse traditions. Frithjof Schuon mentions in this regard notably the Virgin Mary, the Shekhīnah of the Jews, the Pte San Win of the Indians of North America, and the Bodhisattva Avalokiteśvara, identified with the goddess Kuan-Yin in the Far East (1993: 92–93). In the same vein, Jesus, speaking of himself, says: 'Verily, verily, I say unto you, before Abraham was, I am' (John 8: 58). And Muhammad: 'I was a Prophet when Adam was still between water and clay.'

In this way Kuntī identifies Kṛṣṇa as the Lord (*īśvara*, etymologically the Owner, the Almighty, the Master), in perfect congruity with the terminology of *bhakti* according to which the devotee thus names his chosen deity (*iṣṭa-devatā*). It goes without saying that it is Kṛṣṇa exclusively who plays the role of *īśvara* in the epic and it is also true that by force of circumstances, the contemporaries of an avatar do not really have any choice; the *iṣṭa-devatā* imposes itself on all those who have the rare privilege of living in direct proximity to such a theophany. But we know that nowadays, in Hinduism, the faithful may choose to address to any divinity of the pantheon, or to a particular aspect of one of them, the exclusive worship due to God Himself. The choice of an *iṣṭa-devatā* depends on family tradition, the recommendation of a guru, or personal affinity. Whatever the reason, the deity in question then becomes God Himself for the devotee, in the monotheistic sense of the word, with the subtle difference that for the Hindu, there is no problem if a member of his religion or even someone outside his own tradition worships another divine person.[2] This deity then assumes the role of personal God to whom he addresses his prayers and who opens to him the way to *brahman*, the Absolute Reality. In today's practice, the followers of the *sanātana-dharma* are in fact currently divided into three groups according to whether they worship a form of Viṣṇu, Śiva or Devī, which comprise the Vaishnavite, Śaivite and Śaktic or Tantric sects respectively. The first god of the classical *trimūrti* (the triple divine manifestation), Brahmā, has, however, at least in principle, no devotees. It seems paradoxical to Hindus to invoke the Creator when the precise purpose of the way is to leave the world; that is to say, to reverse somehow the process of creation. It may be noted, finally, that it is this term *īśvara* which is the exact and correct equivalent of the word God in

---

[2] Hindus are only polytheists in a very relative sense, and the missionaries who criticized them for it obviously missed the point.

translations of the Bible into Sanskrit. *Credo in unum Deum*: I believe in one *īśvara*.[3]

Kuntī then says that Kṛṣṇa is beyond nature (*prakṛti*), in the sense that *puruṣa*, the Primordial Man, is not 'affected' by *prakṛti*. Hence he is manifest in the world *a priori*, as indiscernible, indistinguishable (*alakṣya*, without a distinctive feature), because nothing differentiates him at first sight from other men. The avatar appears to go *incognito* and cannot be recognized except by 'those who have eyes to see and ears to hear'. But a full awareness of the infinitude of the divine being can only be achieved in a kind of mystical ecstasy, as is the case when Arjuna contemplates his companion and charioteer in his cosmic form on the eve of the battle, as reported in chapter 11 of the *Bhagavad-gītā*, or when Yaśodā sees that her adopted son, still a toddler, has eaten some earth in play, and on asking him to open his mouth to clean it, discovers within it the vastness of the universe. Although the name Kṛṣṇa means midnight blue, there is nothing in the epic to suggest that his contemporaries saw him thus, and it is only in iconography that Kṛṣṇa is shown with a dark blue skin that distinguishes him from ordinary men. It is the colour of Viṣṇu, black like a cloud heavy with rain, or like the deep blue sky. This colour is definitely tamasic, that is to say, it expresses *a priori* a tendency to obscure manifestation. But we must not forget that the three *guṇa*, the fundamental qualities of nature, are intimately bound up, symbolized by Śiva's tresses or his

[3] For devotees whose *iṣṭa-devatā* is Devī under one or another of her aspects, *īśvara* becomes *īśvarī*. This means that the word for God, in the usual sense of the term, can equally be feminine in the Indian tradition.

trident. To illustrate the interaction of these forces, the *Sāṃkhya* explicitly uses the example of the cloud to show how *tamas* (the cloud that hides the sun) causes *sattva* (the fertilizing rain) and *rajas* (the passionate pain of separated lovers).[4] From a more general point of view, Viṣṇu being *sattva* is white, Brahmā as *rajas* is red, and it is Śiva who as *tamas* is black. To resolve this apparent contradiction Swami Harshananda (1986: 85) explains that Viṣṇu is dark outside and white inside, while Śiva is bright like the snow of the Himalayas and black in the depths of himself. The parity of Viṣṇu and Śiva recalls in this context the *yin yang* symbol of the Far East. As for Indian folk wisdom, it explains Kṛṣṇa's dark blue colour by saying that the avatar is so far away from men that a thick layer of air and sky are between him and us, and that in fact he is really huge, but because of the distance he appears as tall as an ordinary man. A poetical way indeed to describe both the transcendence and the immanence of the avatar.

The Queen lastly notes that Kṛṣṇa is at once within and outside of all creatures, as the Self of all beings, in accordance with the teachings of the *Bhagavad-gītā*: '(*Brahman*) is outside and inside of creatures, it is immobile and mobile. It is so subtle[5] that it cannot be perceived (by the senses), it is far and near' (13, 15). In other words, Kṛṣṇa is both the object and subject of knowledge.[6]

---

4 *Sāṃkhyakārikā*, 12.

5 Subtle: from the Latin *sub tela*, under the veil, at the back of the world, so to speak.

6 Similarly, the Qur'an (57: 3) says, in speaking of God: 'He is the First and the Last, and the Outward and the Inward.'

2. *(I salute thee) in my ignorance, thou who, covered by the veil of illusion, art Adhokṣaja, the Imperishable, who is hidden from the foolish who do not recognise the dancer in his costume.*

Here the Queen describes herself as ignorant, like a fool incapable of recognizing a dancer in costume. This confession is paradoxical insofar as she seems fully aware of the real nature of the person to whom she is speaking, but it indicates the limit of the knowledge of God from a still individual point of view. In a very fine passage, Fernand Brunner, who was the present writer's professor of philosophy, seems to be commenting on this verse when he writes: 'Ignorance is the human contribution to the knowledge of God (...). If the knowledge of God can only be divine, it is necessarily ignorance from the point of view of man. It is therefore futile to aspire to the knowledge of God based on our limited individuality; the problem of the knowledge of God put in this fashion has no solution: God and the individual are opposed to each other. But who can oppose God? Therefore we must remove the effects of thought at its source and learn, by confessing God to be unknowable, to abandon the limited individuality' (1954: 201). The avatar is thus paradoxically immersed in the world of illusion (*māyā*) of which he is the Master, and only deliverance (*mokṣa*) permits one to know him for what he really is and not in a merely theoretical fashion.

Kṛṣṇa is then called Adhokṣaja, which we have not translated since it is a proper name which has several different meanings. When still an infant, Kṛṣṇa was suckled by the terrible demoness Pūtanā, who had put poison in her breast milk, and the divine baby not only destroyed the effects of the venom, but sucked the life force out of this false nurse and killed her. The villagers then named him Adhokṣaja, in other words, 'He who is born (again) in his cradle.' It is interesting to note that, according to the *Bhāgavata-purāṇa* (10, 6, 34), when Pūtanā's body was burned on the pyre, a scent of sandalwood rose into the air, and just like Kaṃsa as discussed above, the demoness was instantly delivered from all sin by the mere fact of having been killed by the avatar.

In addition, Adhokṣaja is also one of the twenty-four principal names of Viṣṇu, meaning 'He who holds the discus in his lower (left) hand.' Viṣṇu has in this context only twenty-four names (and not a thousand), corresponding to all the mathematically possible combinations of the four symbols he brandishes in his four arms: the lotus, conch, mace and discus. The ambivalence of the translation comes from the word *akṣa*, wheel, which designates either through synecdoche a cradle on wheels, or through metonymy the discus *(cakra)*, which is a circular weapon. In addition, in Krishnaite theology, Viṣṇu Adhokṣaja is invariably described as *atīndriya*, that is to say, 'He who is beyond the perception of the senses,' which offers yet another meaning to the name in question.

Lastly, the metaphor of the dancer *(naṭa)* is recurrent in Indian symbolism. It is, in this regard, especially Śiva who is considered the Lord of the dance (Naṭarājan), a cosmic dance which represents the unfolding of the universe. But Kṛṣṇa also dances on many occasions, such as with the gopis or on the head of the serpent Kāliya, whom he neutralizes with disconcerting ease while still a child, to rid the frightened villagers of him. In this verse, however, the dance manifests the avatar's power of *māyā*, which is able to mislead fools, and as we saw above, in the epic, many are the individuals who, like ordinary men obsessed with their worldly preoccupations, are unable to even theoretically discern the divine Reality behind the veil of illusion.[7]

3. *How can we women know thee, (who came to earth) to teach the path of devotion to the wise and pure of heart, (destined) for the highest realization* (parama-haṃsa)*?*

Kuntī humbly refers here to a prejudice which excluded women from any real participation in gnosis. In fact, this section of humanity was not alone in suffering a certain ostracism by the Brahmins at a time of hardening in the tradition that preceded the emergence of *bhakti*. That is why in the *Bhagavad-gītā* Kṛṣṇa has to make Arjuna understand: 'O son of Pṛthā-Kuntī, those who take refuge in me, whether they be men of low birth, women, *vaiśya* or even *śūdra*, also reach the supreme goal' (9, 32). Even women of noble birth were equated with the lower castes, since being deprived of initiation, they had no access to the privileges enjoyed by Brahmins; but the role of the avatar is to always redress the balance, wherever *dharma* falters in the world. One of the most famous verses in the *Bhagavad-gītā* proclaims: 'O descendant of Bharata, whenever *dharma* declines and *adharma* arises, then I manifest myself' (4, 7). There is no question of embarking here on a thorough critique of the status of women in India. Even though there are some matriarchal castes, such as the Nayar of Kerala, or some matriarcal ethnic groups like the Newar in Nepal, it is clear that In-

[7] In *Sāṃkhya-kārikā* (59), it is nature itself (*prakṛti*) that is presented as a dancer.

dian society, along with many others, affords women a low social status, and that most of the fight for the defence of their rights is both legitimate and necessary. But social conditions are one thing and spiritual conditions another. In the present time (that is, in a far more serious state of *adharma* than the era preceding the composition of the *Bhagavad-gītā*), this is attested to by the spiritual influence of several famous women who are considered to have acquired the highest degree of realization such as Mā Ānandamayī (1896–1982) and Mā Amṛtānandamayī (born in 1953), more commonly known as Amma. But to return to the Vedic period, it should be noted that at that time there were among the *ṛṣi*, the sages who passed on the Vedic hymns, a significant number of women (in fact, twenty-seven). Women also played a key role in the major sacrifices conducted in principle by married couples. Finally, we can see in the *Upaniṣad* that women also had access to knowledge and could also play the role of *gurvī* (female *guru*).

Bhakti-yoga,[8] the path of devotion, is therefore aimed at those who are, potentially at least, wise (*muni*), having a pure, or literally spotless, heart. The term *muni* refers in a fairly general way to sages, ascetics and hermits. Monier-Williams, author of the most famous Sanskrit-English dictionary, cites as a probable etymology of the word, that given in an ancient *sūtra*, which derives from the root *MAN*, to think. He glosses it as follows: 'anyone who is moved by inward impulse, an ecstatic or inspired

---

8 In this expression, common to the *Bhāgavata-purāṇa* and the *Bhagavad-gītā*, the word *yoga*, which one may translate as discipline or way, has a broader meaning than it took on later in the *yoga-darśana*.

person, an enthusiast.' It is only in a derivative sense that this word means one who has taken a vow of silence (*mauna*). So he is essentially an automaton in the primary meaning of the word, namely a being who 'moves by itself' without outside influence. 'Liberated from himself and all status, all duties and all rights, he has become a Mover-at-will (*kāmacārī*) like the Spirit (...) which "moveth as it will" (...), and as Saint Paul expresses it, "no longer under the law"' (Coomaraswamy, *Hinduism and Buddhism*, 1971: 18). Mā Ānandamayī, mentioned above, perfectly illustrated this realization on a human level. She constantly moved at the discretion of her will which was completely beyond the logic of those who followed her. In this she illustrated a possibility that was the inverse of that incarnated by the famous Ramaṇa Maharṣi (1879–1950), who spent his entire life in the same place on the hill of Aruṇācala.

The accomplished *muni* is designated in Kuntī's speech as *parama-haṃsa*, the supreme swan, one who has attained the highest realization, a title that was given, *par excellence*, to the famous Bengali saint Rāmakṛṣṇa (1836–1886). The swan (*haṃsa*)[9] moves over the water as if hovering over it, without becoming wet. It also represents discernment, because they say in India that when a container is filled with water and milk, the swan is able to drink only the milk, the symbol of knowledge. At the time of the *kṛta-yuga*, equivalent to the Golden Age of the Greeks, men were all *haṃsa* and therefore formed only one caste (*Bhāgavata-purāṇa*, 11, 17, 10).

[9] This word is related to the English goose, *Gans* in German and *anser* in Latin, as Livy called the famous geese of the Capitol.

Haṃsa (*haṃso* in the nominative form) is still regarded as one of the twelve *mahāvākya*, or great synthetic formulas of the *Upaniṣad*, because the one who keeps repeating this jaculatory prayer, inhaling and exhaling on both syllables, pronounces, as if mirroring it, the axiom of the supreme identity: *so'ham*, 'I am That' (*Haṃsopaniṣad*, 2–4). This invocation merges with the breath uniting the life of the body and the spirit. Sufism, in its sacred dances, also considers the sound of the breath a divine Name. And for the initiated, the death rattle is the last prayer of the man on the verge of rendering up his soul to God.

4. *Homage to thee, Kṛṣṇa, son of Vasudeva and joy of Devakī, homage to Govinda, the young adopted son of the cowherd Nanda.*

Kṛṣṇa is the son of Vasudeva of Yādava lineage and Devakī, the cousin of King Kaṃsa, the usurper. The latter, greedy for power, put his own father, Ugrasena, the legitimate king of Mathurā, in prison. But at Devakī's wedding, a voice from Heaven cursed him, telling him that he would one day be overthrown by one of her sons. Kaṃsa at first decided to kill Devakī, but Vasudeva obtained a partial reprieve for his wife and they were both imprisoned by the wicked king in a common cell, so that they were allowed, despite their disgrace, to engender progeny. Thus six sons were born in captivity, all of whom were immediately killed by the tyrant. When she was pregnant a seventh time, the unfortunate mother miraculously managed to transmit her embryo into the womb of a co-wife, Rohinī, when she came to visit them. Thus, the latter bore Balarāma, the elder brother of Kṛṣṇa, also considered an avatar of Viṣṇu, or more precisely of the serpent Śeṣa, the Remainder, on which the god falls asleep during the nights of Brahmā, between two creations of the world.[10] Finally, when Devakī was pregnant for the eighth time another miracle took place. She gave birth in the middle of the night—for Kṛṣṇa was born at midnight like Jesus—then a supernatural torpor seized the guards, and Vasudeva was able to leave, taking the newborn baby with him out of the jail. He crossed the Yamunā, like Saint Christopher carrying the infant Christ, entrusted the baby to Nanda and Yaśodā, a couple from the cowherd caste, and returned the same night to his wife. The next day Vasudeva and Devakī pretended to Kaṃsa that Devakī had had a miscarriage. Thereafter, a daughter was born while they were still in captivity. But when the king wanted to kill her in turn, out of pure cruelty this time, she escaped from his hands and flew into the air,

---

10 Balarāma is implicitly associated with his brother in eighth place in the list of the ten major incarnations of Viṣṇu. Sometimes it is he who exclusively occupies this place, Kṛṣṇa then occupying the ninth and the Buddha being left out. In the famous Krishnaite invocation borrowed from the *Brahmāṇa-purāṇa* and popularized by Caitanya, *Hare Kṛṣṇa Hare Kṛṣṇa Kṛṣṇa Kṛṣṇa Hare Hare, Hare Rāma Hare Rāma Rāma Rāma Hare Hare*, as in the proper name Rāmakṛṣṇa, Rāma refers to Balarāma and not Rāmacandra in the *Rāmāyaṇa*. There would also be no reason to connect, in such a fundamental invocation, two avatars whose functions are so distinct and who appear in two periods so far removed from each other in time. Similarly, Christians do not invoke Jesus with Moses, for example, but certainly *Iesu-Maria* as being two inseparable aspects of the same avataric reality.

crying out to the king that the child who was to revenge them all had already been born. It was she, Subhadrā, actually an incarnation of *yoga-nidrā*, the Sleep of the mind caused by *yoga*, who became the second wife of Arjuna. Therefore the thwarted Kaṃsa, having no longer any reason to keep his cousin and her husband prisoners, released them without however giving up the search for their son in various ways. The horrible demoness Pūtanā, whom we have already encountered (v. 2), was sent by him.

This episode is obviously striking in its resemblance to the massacre of the innocents perpetrated by Herod, or to the massacre of male children ordered by Pharaoh in order to get rid of Moses, whom the Egyptian astrologers claimed was born to destroy him. One could no doubt allow, as some have done, that the beings sacrificed in this way were mysteriously absorbed into the avatar, somehow increasing his vital energy. This, at least, is the opinion of Ibn 'Arabī, who concludes: '... Moses was then the sum of the lives of those who had been killed with the intention of destroying him' (1975: 96). In a similar vein, Jacobus de Voragine notes in *The Golden Legend* that the Holy Innocents are celebrated in the liturgy, although they are theoretically related to the Old Law, 'because Jesus Christ was killed in each of them' (chapter on the Maccabees).

One may also wonder why Kṛṣṇa was the eighth child born to Vasudeva and Devakī. In Christian symbolism, Jesus was resurrected on the first day of the week, or rather on the eighth, as glossed by commentators, who see it as the beginning of a new cycle after the completion of the Judaic week related to the Mosaic Law.

In the same way, Kṛṣṇa inaugurates a new cycle of the *dharma*. The initiatory value of the number eight, which has a symbolic connection to the musical octave, also explains why baptisteries are generally octogonal[11] constructions. The week was only known in India after the arrival of the Greeks, at the time of Alexander's campaigns in the 4th century BC, but it was appropriated, at least, from the Puranic age onwards.[12] Nonetheless, the language of numbers goes beyond this one plane. Balarāma is the serpent Śeṣa, that is to say he embodies what remains of previous cycles and implicitly summarizes all the previous incarnations of Viṣṇu, as 'he represents all the individual souls (*jīva*) in their subtle form, which are residues of the previous cycle, which need new opportunities for rebirth' (Swami Harshananda 1986: 53).[13] In this respect, his function is reminiscent of John the Baptist, the cousin of Jesus who was six months older than him, and who ensured in his own way the link between the world of the Old Testament and that of the New. Lastly, the number eight represents, for India as a whole, a cosmic totality symbolized by the eight petals of the lotus, signifying the eight directions of space, namely the

---

11 In the same way, eight people repopulated the world after the flood, Noah, his wife, their three sons and their wives. The Jews meanwhile celebrate a jubilee every fifty years, that is to say, after seven times seven years; the fiftieth inaugurates a new cycle.

12 As attested to in the *Śiva-purāṇa*, for example, 14, 20–22.

13 In the microcosmic context of *Yoga*, *Śeṣa* is the *kuṇḍalinī*, the *śakti* of Śiva, wound like a snake at the bottom of the spine and waiting to be awakened (see Michael 1980: 187).

four cardinal and four intermediary points.[14] The claim of the Krishnaites who see in Kṛṣṇa the only truly full incarnation of Viṣṇu, is perfectly consistent with this appreciation of the number eight.

In the verse that concerns us, Kṛṣṇa is called Vāsudeva, that is to say 'son of Vasudeva, the Bright (or Beneficial) Celestial[15] Being', with an elongation of the first a, which indicates lineage. But this word Vāsudeva is glossed (*Bhāgavata-purāṇa*, 4, 3, 23) as 'pure virtue' (*sattvaṃ viśuddham*) and, insofar as it refers to the fundamental reality buried in man's heart, it can substitute any other proper name in common usage. In the same way Muslims call anyone whose name they do not know 'Muhammad' without distinction. Now, to name the avatar by his patronym is to signify his entry into the world of men, into history, be it ever so mythical. The descent (of the god into the world), since this is the etymological sense of the word *avatāra*, is further materialized and sealed in this case by an adoption. Like Moses and Muhammad, Kṛṣṇa is adopted and what is more, by a member of the *vaiśya* community, namely the cowherd caste. We spoke earlier of a popularization of religion. In fact, Rāma in the second age and Kṛṣṇa at

---

14 For some philologists, the number eight, *aṣṭa* (*octo*), is a dual form of the number four, *catur* (*quattuor*). The wheel which symbolizes traditional Indian space can be further subdivided into 16 rays, all governed by a tutelary god. See in this regard, for example, the summary by Michel Angot (2001: 101–3).

15 We have translated here the word *deva* as heavenly being. If this term is etymologically related to the Latin *deus* it is often ambiguous to translate it by the word god. Coomaraswamy systematically renders it as angel.

the junction of the third and fourth are *kṣatriya* in origin, which already marks a departure from the brahmanical norm. But we see here that it was necessary that the latter be welcomed among the lowliest castes, that he might grow up and live among them, so that his message would spread to all. In a hardly different, symbolic fashion, Jesus himself was also adopted by Joseph who belonged to the royal line of David and Solomon, and was born 'accidentally' in Bethlehem and not Nazareth. Indeed it was necessary, according to divine Providence, that he be registered in the census of the Roman Empire, and as a result 'counted' among men and thus even introduced into what Guénon calls 'the reign of quantity'.

It is in these circumstances therefore that Kṛṣṇa earns the title of Govinda, the Guardian of the cows (*go*), and in India this humble function is never considered a punishment, as is the case with Apollo doomed to become the cattle minder of Admetus. It is hardly necessary to recall in this regard the importance of the cow in Indian ritual, symbol *par excellence* of Mother Earth and also of the Voice fertilized by the breath (the bull) and giving birth to thought (the calf), as recounted in *Bṛhadāraṇyakopaniṣad* (5, 8, 1). But traditional scholars also give the name Govinda the hermeneutic meaning of Guardian of the senses, which we will return to later.

5. *Homage to thee, O lotus-navelled One, homage to thee, who wearest garlands of lotus, homage to thee the lotus-eyed, homage to thee, the soles of whose feet bear the mark of the lotus.*

Sanskrit contains a great many words to describe the word lotus, much to the joy of poets who thus have at their disposal a certain leeway to meet the demands of metric versification, but not all these words are pure synonyms; each of them has its own etymology. Now, here Kuntī insists on using the same word *paṅkaja* four times. *Paṅkaja* is the one who is born (*-ja*) in the mud (*paṅka*). We understand then that this word is not chosen at random. It symbolizes the avatar who graciously, indeed miraculously, reclines on the mud of the world without being defiled, which is consistent with the spatial symbolism that we discussed in the previous verse. But before going into the details of the description of Kṛṣṇa given by the Queen, the extreme elegance of the order of the enumeration of his physical attributes should be noted. Although in the family hierarchy Kuntī, as Kṛṣṇa's aunt, is senior to him, she addresses her nephew as a humble devotee. First she gazes at him with eyes lowered to the height of his navel, then she raises her head, first to see his neck, then his eyes, and finally she bows her head to focus her attention on his feet. In poetry in general, when describing a person, we will in principle go from top to bottom, from head to toe, starting with the hair. This diversion from the rule illustrates the exceptional quality in the inspiration of this text.

The lotus, besides the conch, discus and mace, is one of the four major attributes of Viṣṇu. While it symbolizes his purity, it also, more specifically, represents his ability to incarnate, to bloom, like a celestial flower in the world. The allusion to the lotus of the navel refers to the myth of Viṣṇu lying on the serpent Śeṣa (the Remainder) or Ananta (Infinity), who comes out of his dream and wakes up at the end of the cosmic night. A lotus with a long stem emerges from his navel in the form of a bud. Then it opens, and Brahmā, the Creator with four heads, appears in the flower, ready to create a new world. This scene is one of the most frequently represented in traditional iconography. The lotus garland adorning the neck of the god thus symbolizes the multiplicity of worlds, created in a sequence similar to that of a pearl necklace or rosary. Concerning the lotuses of his eyes, they reflect his benevolence or his power to seduce souls, but there are also terrible forms of Viṣṇu where the eyes are covered to neutralize their destructive power, such as those of the Veṅkiteśvara of Tirupati.[16] The devotee, through humility, also worships the lotus appearing on the soles of Viṣṇu/Kṛṣṇa's feet. The foot is the contact point between Heaven and Earth, between the Kingdoms above and below, and its imprint is a sign of the presence of the divinity in the world. Now those of the avatar stay free from the dust of the world. In a famous fable from the *Mahābhārata*, the beautiful Damayantī recognizes her human lover, Nala, amongst a number of gods who have taken on his appearance in order to seduce her. She thwarts their ruse by noticing that dust does not adhere to their feet, they do not sweat, and their eyes do not blink, unlike Nala who is a mere mortal.

6. *O Master of the senses, O Omnipresent Lord, just as the long-imprisoned Devakī tormented by the wicked Kaṃsa, was*

---

[16] Tirumala temple, near Tirupati in southern Andhra Pradesh, attracts thousands of pilgrims every day, including a considerable number of Christians and Muslims. One visits Lord Veṅkita to free oneself of one's sins. It should be noted that for some, Veṅkita is a form of Śiva.

released by thee, have I, with my sons, been released from countless misfortunes thanks to thy protection.

In this verse Kṛṣṇa is first of all named Hṛṣīkeśa, the Master of the senses (*hṛṣīka_īśa*), or as is sometimes interpreted by splitting the word up differently (*hṛṣī-keśa*), one whose hair (stands on end with) joy. The holy city of Rishikesh, situated on the Ganges at the foot of the Himalayas, is dedicated to him. The word used here for the senses comes from a root denoting a state of excitement, expectation, even impatience, and at the same time rejoicing. This name of the Master of the senses is in fact susceptible to a double interpretation. The avatar, in his guise as a mere mortal, immersed in the world 'according to the flesh' in the words of Saint Paul (Rom. 9:5), gives a perfect example of mastery of the senses. Thus the gopis who, thanks to their charms, are capable of subjugating even Madana, the god of love, have no more power over Kṛṣṇa's senses than does *prakṛti* have over Īśvara (*Bhāgavata-purāṇa*, 1, 11, 36ff.). But on a deeper level, Hṛṣīkeśa is also the master of our own senses, for insofar as he represents the hidden Self buried in each individual, he acts through all beings.[17] This the misguided (*vimūḍha*) do not perceive. But for the fully conscious realized being, the Self becomes the unique agent. Kṛṣṇa says:

> 'A particle of Myself, the eternal, has become a living soul in the world of the living, attracting the five senses located in nature (*prakṛti*) and the

17 See 'So we being many are one body in Christ, and every one members one of another' (Rom. 12:5), and 'know ye not that your bodies are members of Christ?' (1 Cor. 6:15).

> mind (*manas*). When the Lord (*īśvara*) enters a body then leaves, he takes them with him, as the wind carries away the scent from an incense burner. Having taken possession of the hearing, sight, touch, taste, smell and the mind, he enjoys sense objects for himself' (*Bhagavad-gītā*, 15, 7–9).

This truth is also beautifully illustrated in the Islamic tradition, in a famous *ḥadīth qudsī*, a non-Qur'ānic utterance in which God speaks in the first person through the mouth of the Prophet: 'My servant ceases not to draw nigh unto me until I love him, then I am the hearing with which he hears, the sight with which he sees, the hand with which he grasps and the foot on which he walks.' God is thus the Master of the senses of his servant.

An unreferenced quotation by Swami Prabhupāda states: *hṛṣīkena hṛṣīkeśa-sevanaṃ bhaktirucyate*, 'Devotion through the senses towards the Master of the senses is called *bhakti*.' The term *sevana*, a typical expression of *bhakti*, means devotion, service, and worship. And the same author further recounts this very beautiful verse: 'Whoever, in any circumstances whatsoever, totally dedicates himself to the service of Hari (another name for Kṛṣṇa), in his actions, thoughts and words is a liberated living being (*jīvanmukta*).' The word translated in this passage by the word 'service' is particularly strong, since it means slavehood (*dāsya*) properly so called. Unlike the *jñānin*, who follows the path of knowledge leading to direct union with the divinity, the *bhakta* follows the path of devotion, and remains the servant, the slave of the divinity, abandoning all self-will or egoism. However, in behaving in this way the *bhakta* actually permits the divine spirit to act within him, while the *jñānin* that identifies *a priori* with the spirit strips his will *de facto* of all selfishness. Both ways meet and so it is in this sense that Saint Paul, in an admirably synthetic formula, can conclude: 'I live; yet not I, but Christ liveth in me' (Gal. 2:20).

As for the second term used by the Queen, the Omnipresent (*vibhu*), it means he who penetrates everywhere, who manifests his power in all beings. We have seen above the tragic fate of Devakī and her final liberation. The main tribulations Queen Kuntī has just referred to will now be discussed in the following verse.

7. *O Hari, thou hast already saved us from poison, a great fire, a threatening man-eater, a humiliating gathering, the torments of exile in the forest, and then in battle after battle, the countless darts hurled by great warriors, and, finally, Droṇa's son's weapon.*

Hari is a very common name for Kṛṣṇa, meaning fawn-coloured, or yellow, which is a reference to the colour of his clothes.[18] The poison referred to was given to Bhīma, Kuntī's second son, by his cousin Duryodhana. The great fire refers to the 'House of Lacquer', a house built in order to destroy the Pāṇḍava and their mother, which they fled from thanks to a tunnel they had dug on

---

[18] This term is etymologically related, via the Indo-European (and despite appearances), to *fulvus* in Latin, *gelb* in German and the English yellow. To translate it as 'He who takes away,' as do some, is probably to confuse it with Hara, a name of Śiva that has precisely this meaning. In the expression *Hare Kṛṣṇa*, the two names of the avatar, which curiously refer to two colours, are in the vocative.

the advice of their uncle Vidura. The man-eater was the demon Hiḍimba who fought Bhīma, who had seduced his sister. The humiliating gathering was that of the winners of the dice game whereby the Kaurava caused the fall of the Pāṇḍava and forced them into exile. The mention of the battles and exploits of great warriors refers not only to the major conflict of the eighteen days of Kurukṣetra, but also to the different skirmishes in which the two groups had previously fought along with certain of their allies. As for Droṇa's son Aśvatthāman's weapon, this was the *brahmāstra* that Kṛṣṇa destroyed in order to save Parikṣit. We will focus on the last three of these trials in starting with the famous dice game that occupies such an important place in the epic.

In the *Mahābhārata*, the gods, or at least their incarnations, are constantly playing dice. They do so in a way belying Einstein, who claimed in a famous formula that 'God does not play dice.' Thus Yudhiṣṭhira, the son of the god Dharma and the head of the Pāṇḍava clan, has an unhealthy passion for this game. He cannot refuse Duryodhana's invitation to a friendly game in the presence of all the important people at Dhṛtarāṣṭra's court. However, at the last moment the treacherous Kaurava offers his place to his uncle Śakuni, whose reputation for cheating is well known. But Yudhiṣṭhira cannot and will not hold himself back any longer, and so the game begins. It is not long before this purportedly 'friendly' game turns into a terrible tragedy. The unfortunate Pāṇḍava, forced to bid without limit, eventually loses, after his wealth, his army and his kingdom, his own brothers, himself and his wife. The order of this list is not without significance. For the astute Draupadī, after the attempted humiliation inflicted on her by Duryodhana, argues at the arbitration by king Dhṛtarāṣṭra that her husband having previously lost himself, and as a result become the slave of his opponent, was no longer legitimately able to wager her. Confused by this argument, the blind old man proposes, by way of compensation, to grant her a boon. The young woman demands the release of Yudhiṣṭhira. The king grants her this and requests her to name a second boon. She then asks for the release of her four other husbands. Despite the sovereign's offer of another favour, she refuses according to *dharma* to formulate a third wish and the five Pāṇḍava and their wife-in-common go into exile for twelve years.

The simplest explanation for this passion that the gods have for dice, surprising as it is at first sight, is that their relationships and their intentions escape the grasp of ordinary understanding which sees them as haphazard. But 'chance is the logic of God', says in substance Bernanos (*Dialogue of the Carmelites*, t. 3, s. 1) and this is what lies behind the practice of divination to which we alluded at the beginning of this book, like all consultations of auguries in the traditional worlds. Indeed, in the context of the experience of common men, God 'does what he wants,' to quote the Qur'ān, and His ways generally remain unfathomable to us mortals who do not know his intentions with regard to us. In asserting that God does not play dice, Einstein was correct only 'upstream' of this divine play, referring to a necessity of which the intrinsic logic escapes ordinary people.

In addition, to better understand this traditional point of view, it is interesting to note that the word *deva*, from the root DIV, meaning to shine, is, as we have seen, the equivalent of the Latin *deus*. But the second meaning of this root is to throw the dice.[19] Madeleine Biardeau even suggests a translation of the name of Kṛṣṇa's mother, Devakī, as 'Player of the Dice', which some episodes of her life do indeed seem to justify. One witnesses, what is more, in this famous dice game, a kind of transmission of power between Śakuni, the cheater who plays on behalf of his nephew and is regarded as an incarnation of the *dvāpara-yuga*, the third age, and Duryodhana who incarnates the *kali-yuga*, the fourth age, that of the worst throw of the dice. Cheating, which has become one of the most striking symptoms of the dark age in which we currently find ourselves, was thus already there as a seed in the preceding one. The episode of the game of dice is, in the *Mahābhārata*, the most obvious expression of the role that deception is likely to play in the last age when men seek to deceive *dharma* by putting themselves in the place of Providence, so to speak. In the *Aeneid* there is also a kind of cheating, namely in the episode of the Trojan horse, that decides the outcome of the war marking the transition between the Bronze Age and the Iron Age. One may wonder how

[19] In old French the word for gods (*les dieux*), can be written in the plural *des* and becomes then a homonym for the word dice which has another etymology, since it comes from the Latin *datum*, that which has been given (by lots). When Rutebeuf said that, 'in the tavern the *des* have made me lose,' he expresses himself in an ambivalent way. In Greek the word *daimon* also contains this ambivalence. It is the deity who assigns to every man his share, and the expression *kata daimona*, 'according to the gods' (Herodotus), is translated by 'at random'. Finally, the word hazard, which in Arabic signifies the die, comes also, strangely, from a root meaning to shine (*zahara*).

a ruse that seems so crude to us men of the 21st century, who have become suspicious by nature, could have deceived the Trojans, who might well have suspected, as their priest Laocoon did, that there were soldiers hidden in the wooden contraption. But just like Yudhiṣṭhira, they were men representing the third age, imbued with a naivety which, basically, was to their credit, because it reflected the sensitivity and imagination of a civilization still viscerally attached to the values of honesty and chivalry, even in the context of war. A similar naivety would likewise cause the loss of many traditional peoples still faithful to the given word who were victims of the deceit of the white man, like the Aztecs and Native Americans of North America, for example, who faced a brutal descending cyclic transition.[20] But 'God schemed and He is the best of those who scheme' (Qur'ān 3:54, trad. Pickthall), and we will see later (v. 12) how Kṛṣṇa responds to the deep seated cunning of the men of the last times.

In the rest of the verse, after mentioning the exile in the forest, Kuntī speaks of the great warriors, literally 'those who have a great chariot', that her sons had to face in battle. This pays implicit tribute firstly to those who fought on the wrong side against their will because of their irrevocable allegiance, such as Bhīṣma

---

20 In his 'Reflections on Naivety', Frithjof Schuon (1965: 102ff.) has magisterially treated this problem, explicitly referring to the traditional doctrine of the cycles. He also notes this timeless truth: 'How could a man who is unaware of the existence of falsehood, or who knows it only as a deadly and exceptional sin, appear as otherwise ingenuous to a mean-spirited and artful society?'

or Droṇa, and secondly, to her own son Karṇa, especially bitter towards Arjuna, since the latter refused to fight against him because of his apparent status as a common charioteer. This humiliating rejection was the cause of the son of Sūrya's allegiance to the Kaurava and his fierce hatred towards his brother.

As for the reference to the son of Droṇa, this refers really to a relative protection, as Aśvatthāman, before attacking Parikṣit, killed not only many fighters from the victorious clan in their sleep, but also the five sons of Draupadī. Kṛṣṇa thus saved from peril only their five respective fathers, the Pāṇḍava. Following this criminal act, Aśvatthāman fell into the hands of Arjuna who, on the order of Kṛṣṇa, was about to kill him. But the magnanimous Draupadī, out of respect for the mother of the murderer of her sons, the wife of the guru of her husbands, showed a marvelous clemency towards him and asked for his release, which the avatar granted her, knowing full well that Aśvatthāman would later seek to complete his revenge by attacking Parikṣit, still in the womb of his mother, Uttarā.

8. *May these misfortunes be continuously repeated again and again, O Lord of the world. May thy manifestation, O Lord, put an end to the repetition of births.*

Kuntī's prayer may seem paradoxical, but it is the prayer of a person who is perfectly aware of the initiatory value of the tribulations of this world. Paul once asked the Lord to remove a 'thorn' he had in his flesh three times. But God replied: 'My grace is sufficient for thee: for my strength is made perfect in weakness.' And the Apostle continues: 'Most gladly therefore will I rather glory in my infirmities, that the power of Christ may rest upon me. Therefore I take pleasure in infirmities, in reproaches, in necessities, in persecutions, in distresses for Christ's sake: for when I am weak, then am I strong' (2 Cor. 12: 9–10, KJV). One of the names of Kṛṣṇa, moreover, is Dīnabandhu, that is to say, the Friend (or Relative) of the afflicted, and the Sermon on the Mount also magnifies those who accept their afflictions in the life of the world. It is significant and logical that the Queen thus addresses Kṛṣṇa as Master (*guru*) of the world (*jagat*), who by his teaching delivers us from the miseries of existence. *Jagadguru* is synonymous with *Jagannātha*, the name especially given to Viṣṇu at the temple in Puri, one of his four major dwelling-places (*catur-dhāma*), located in the four corners of India.[21] Indians have two main words for describing the world: *jagat*, that which goes, moves, and *saṃsāra*, that which flows. In the first case as in the second, it is impermanence that is alluded to, and the World Guru teaches his devotees exactly how to overcome this impermanence and find release from the world. The masters of the fivefold lineage of the famous guru Śaṅkara (7th century), the founder of the school of Vedānta, still bear this title today. In contrast, it is notable that the Greeks and Latins saw primarily the beauty of the world and not its illusory nature: the word *cosmos* means etymologically order, as opposed to chaos, and the word *mundus* means that which is pure. As for

---

[21] These dwelling-places are Puri in the east, Rameshvaram in the south, Dwarka in the west, and Badrinath in the north, which is the order they are traditionally cited in, turning in a *pradakṣiṇa*, clock-wise direction.

the Stoics, they would make this beauty of the world one of the proofs for the existence of God.

The second part of this verse is particularly difficult to translate. Kuntī uses a polite form in the third person singular, which could be rendered word for word by: 'May the vision of Your Lordship be the vision of the non-repetition of births.' The translation we have chosen loses the play on the repetition of the word vision (*darśana*) and thus needs a commentary. In India great importance is attached to *darśana*, the experience of seeing a holy person, a statue dedicated in a temple, a landscape or a remarkable site. The beneficiary of this vision derives a special blessing which can in some cases guide him for his entire life. In this respect the contemporaries of an avatar enjoy a unique privilege, as they are in direct contact with his sanctifying presence. But those who are not so lucky are not left unprovided for, as they have a powerful way to fill this gap by remembrance (*smaraṇa*), which has the ability to grant bliss 'to those who have not seen, and yet have believed,' in the words of Jesus. 'Some, not knowing (the truth) by themselves, worship having heard from others. They too triumph over death, taking as the ultimate goal (*parāyaṇa*) what they have heard (*śruti*)' (*Bhagavad-gītā*, 13, 25). In the case of Kṛṣṇa, it is especially his flute playing that causes this *smaraṇa*: the gopis, the milkmaids, who represent the human soul, all fall in love with the adolescent god on hearing his music without even seeing him. But more importantly, it is on hearing his name that they experience divine ecstasy, as in this beautiful Bengali poem by Suren Goshai, in which Rādhā, in love with Kṛṣṇa, addresses her friend Lalitā:

Kṛṣṇa! What a marvellous name!
O Lalitā, this name has only two syllables, but what honey is hidden in this name!

All my senses are captivated by it.
My heart falls in love with the one name of Kṛṣṇa.
My tongue wants to taste this honey.

My ear thirsts to hear his name again and again.
Thousands of invocations of the name cannot satisfy it.
My eyes are eager to see him.

If his name is so powerful what will his company be like?
My lips move constantly in chanting his name.

[translated by Parvathy Baul]

In fact, according to traditional teaching, Kṛṣṇa or Rāma or any other of these major theophanies are mysteriously fully present in their name. This reality is the foundation of the continuous practice of the invocation of the divine Names regardless of religion, which is considered the most effective spiritual path for the times we live in. Kṛṣṇadāsa Kavirāja, a biographer of Caitanya from the early 17th century, says, 'In the *kali-yuga*, Kṛṣṇa is incarnate in His name' (*Caitanya-caritāmṛta*, *Ādi*, 17, 22, quoted by Swami Prabhupāda 1990: 99). Like many other masters Rāmakṛṣṇa, also emphasizes the virtue of the Name, and recalls an anecdote involving two of Kṛṣṇa's wives: 'Why, is the name a trifling thing? God is not different from His Name. Satyabhāmā tried to balance Krishna with gold and precious stones but could not do it. Then Rukminī put a *tulsi* leaf with the name of

Kṛṣṇa on the scales. That balanced the Lord' (M., translated by Swami Nikhilananda, 1942: 386). The craft of the epic in employing anecdotes for spiritual purposes is here unsurpassed.

In the *Bhagavad-gītā* Kṛṣṇa says: 'He who really knows my birth and my divine action (*karman*), is not born again on departing his body, but comes to me, O Arjuna' (4, 9). It is not at all here a question of reincarnation in the ordinary sense of the word, of the periodic reappearance on earth of a given individual over the centuries,[22] for all this must be understood in a metaphorical, or better still, an anagogical sense, as defined in the West by the medieval exegetes of Scripture. Certainly there is no shortage of Hindus who literally believe that such and such a person will after his death be reborn in the body of some animal, or Christians who think that one day they will meet Saint Peter in the clouds. But it is necessary to make allowances for this popular imagery and not lose sight of the esoteric meaning of this teaching.[23]

Whoever, therefore, leaves aside his ego and is reborn in Kṛṣṇa through invoking his name, actually (*tattvatas*)

---

22 One also wonders what Sanskrit word could possibly translate the word reincarnation. In the verse which concerns us, Kuntī speaks of *punar-bhava*, that is to say, repeated birth, or rather repeated state.

23 'Need I say that no doctrine of reincarnation, according to which the very being and person of a man who has once lived on earth and is now deceased will be reborn of another terrestrial mother has ever been taught in India...?' and 'We die and are reborn daily and hourly and "death" when the time comes is only a special case' (Coomaraswarmy 1977: 15).

leaves the world and abandons all transience. He becomes timeless and without a future, a true 'son of the moment', to borrow a Sufi formula. This is also the real meaning of the phrase 'to outwit time' (*kāla-vañcana*) as it appears in Tantric literature (Feuerstein 1998: ch. 1, n. 3). 'Outwitting time' only makes sense if by it we mean 'living in the moment'.

9. *The man drunk with arrogance because of his birth, his power, his learning or his beauty is unable to submit to thee, who art a pasture for those who have nothing.*

The second part of this verse is a perfect example of the inadequacies of an univocal translation. Certainly to translate is to interpret, and above we have opted for the version nearest to etymology. But here is how we can also understand the key words of this sentence. Firstly, the verb *arhati* can be rendered as to deserve. The arrogant are not only unable to submit to the Lord, but they do not deserve to, or perhaps one should rather say that they do not deserve the grace inherent in this submission. Then the second verb, *abhidhātum* (here in the infinitive form), also has another well-known meaning: to name. The arrogant are as incapable of naming the Lord as they are of submitting to him, and, moreover, they do not deserve to. We have seen the importance of invoking the name of Kṛṣṇa. Kuntī says categorically that arrogance deprives a man of the means *par excellence* of sanctification, that is, the invocation of the divine Names. Finally, a pasture (*gocara*) is properly the place where cows graze, but we have also seen that in traditional Indian symbolism cows represent the senses. Pasturage is thus, in its true meaning, that which feeds the cows and metaphorically, that which offers itself as an object to the senses; thus only those who have nothing, and are devoid of all goods engendering self-sufficiency, are the ones who perceive the Lord and rejoice in his paradisal presence.

But let us return to the man rendered drunk and arrogant by his wealth. Most certainly material wealth, including, as here, birth in a high caste, power, learning[24] and physical beauty are only obstacles to the spiritual life according to the measure in which they provoke intoxication, because in themselves these advantages are not necessarily detrimental. This is why Christ could say: 'It is easier for a camel to pass through the eye of a needle, than for a rich man to enter the kingdom of God' (Matthew 19: 24). The more the West, for example, accumulates useless goods which lure it with 'the deceitfulness of riches' (Mark 4: 19), the more it appears to move further away from the spiritual. But hagiography offers no lack of rich men who remained such, and yet attained a high degree of sanctity. We may be surprised to learn that, in the *Bhagavad-gītā* (7, 16), Kṛṣṇa counts as one of the four categories of virtuous men (*sukṛtin*), who worship him without being led astray by illusion, those who seek to acquire wealth legitimately (*arthārthin*). And conversely, material poverty, despite some relative advantages, is itself no guarantee of spiritual elevation, and too often creates bitterness. It is obviously therefore only in an inward sense that one must understand this

---

24 *Śruta*, the same root as *śruti*, is a term that refers *a priori* to sacred knowledge. But in this context it must be seen as a bookish erudition with no real operative value.

teaching. However, in this situation, 'to be poor is to be as God created us without accumulating any guile, or attitude of pride,' writes Frithjof Schuon. And the same author says again, using Sufi terminology: 'There is no *dhikr* without *faqr*.'[25] In other words, to paraphrase Kuntī, you cannot invoke the name of the Lord in a manner which is both worthy of Him and effective without first getting rid of the arrogance and intoxication that grow like weeds out of our innate gifts, or out of the riches we have acquired in this world, and which in effect prevent God naming Himself within us and through us.

Another word on the metaphor of pasture, for Kṛṣṇa is a shepherd like Jesus, who portrays himself as such in several parables. The latter also says: 'I am the door: by me if any man enter in, he shall be saved, and shall go in and out, and find pasture' (John 10: 9). At a time when serious conflicts have arisen between different religious communities, such doctrinal, symbolic and metaphorical convergences between Hinduism, Christianity and Islam deserve to be highlighted more than ever.

10. *I salute Him who is the wealth of those who have nothing, the One whose existence is independent of the fundamental qualities of the world. I salute Him who finds his joy in himself, who is peaceful, the Master of the monists.*

Concerning once more the idea of those who have nothing, who possess nothing (*akiñcana* with a privat-

25 Unpublished texts. *Dhikr* is the Arabic equivalent of *smaraṇa*, the remembrance of God as seen above. As for *faqr*, it is spiritual poverty, hence the name *faqīr* that Sufis call themselves, which means the poor.

ive *a*-), even though we have argued that this is necessarily a spiritual and not a material poverty, it should be recalled that many of the heroes of the epic, for example, are immensely rich, whether it be a question of Kṛṣṇa who is the king of Dvārakā (modern Dwarka) or the Pāṇḍava, once they have recovered their kingdom. But in the spiritual realm, the *iṣṭa-devatā* is the exclusive wealth which supersedes and replaces all others, such as in the well-known Gospel parable: 'The Kingdom of Heaven is like unto a merchant seeking goodly pearls: who, when he had found one pearl of great price, went and sold all that he had, and bought it' (Matthew 13:45–46). In addition, the wealth which we must renounce is by no means all material. The *Bhagavad-gītā* is replete with exhortations towards non-attachment (*asakti, anabhiṣaṅga*), either to desire or hatred, pleasure or pain, and even to one's own home, wife and children, with a view to an exclusive and unceasing union with the Self (13, 5–11).[26] It advocates primarily that we should perfectly forego the fruits of our actions, which must be performed according to our nature, but selflessly (12, 10–12). Rāmakṛṣṇa saw in this attitude the essence of the sacred text, to the point that he heard in the repetition of the word *gītā gītā gītā*, the word *tāgī tāgī* which he interpreted as a variant of *tyāgī*, the renouncer (in Swami Chidbhavananda 1969: 66). And: 'Know, O Pāṇḍava, that this path (that

26 See 'If any man come to me and hate not his father, and mother, and wife, and children, and brethren, and sisters, yea, and his own life also, he cannot be my disciple' (Luke 14:26, KJV), and 'O ye who believe! Lo! Among your wives and children there are enemies for you' (Qur'ān 64:14, trans. Pickthall). Kuntī says the same thing in verse 24.

of *dhyāna-yoga*, the yoga of meditation) is said to be renunciation (*saṃnyāsa*). No one becomes a *yogin* who has not renounced desire (*saṃkalpa*)'[27] (*Bhagavad-gītā*, 6, 2).

With regard to the overall meaning of the verse, although its beginning is sufficiently explicit in the form we have given it, we can also translate it equally satisfactorily as: 'I salute Him who is known (only) by those who have nothing.' This ambivalence is inherent in the root *VID*, which means not only to see and to know, but also to acquire.[28] Following this salutation, Kuntī affirms the transcendence of the person of Kṛṣṇa in several ways. First of all, He is that which is independent of the world defined as the interaction of the three *guṇa* or fundamental tendencies. We have already mentioned this word above (v. 1) in relation to *prakṛti*, nature. But here the *guṇa* are mentioned explicitly, which obliges us to consider them further. The meaning of the term *guṇa* is string, particularly the bow string which provides the impetus for the arrow's flight. Fired upwards, the arrow is *sattva*, that is to say, conforming to being. As such, it therefore represents the luminous, clear quality characteristic of the pure sky and the ether.[29] *Rajas* is the arrow fired horizontally; it is colourful

---

27 '*Saṃkalpa* is the selfish motive behind an action. It is actuated by desire' (Swami Chidbhavananda, 1969: 358).

28 In both cases, the past participle is *vitta*. But in the second meaning, the verb takes in the rest of the conjugation an infix *n*, as in the words *finden* in German and find in English, which have the same origin as *videre* in Latin. Govinda is therefore, etymologically, he who acquires or finds cows, rather than one who sees them or guards them.

29 *Sat* is the present participle of the verb to be (*AS*).

and relatively opaque like the atmosphere, and it then represents the dynamic and expansive tendency. Fired downwards, it is *tamas*, the dark tendency, representing inertia and gravitation.[30] The field of action of these arrows embraces the three worlds of the Earth, the Atmosphere and Heaven, to which the famous Vedic invocation *bhūr-bhuvaḥ svaḥ* refers in particular. From the point of view of man, that is to say, not from the macrocosmic but from the microcosmic perspective, these three trends correspond to virtue, passion and vice, or to intelligence, discursive reason and ignorance. It is in the *darśana*, the philosophical school of *Sāṃkhya*, that this doctrine of the constituent qualities of the created world finds its most comprehensive and explicit expression.

Kṛṣṇa is then described as *ātmārāma*, the One who finds his joy in Himself, and is sufficient unto himself. This other aspect of transcendence shows how he who takes refuge in Him, and Him alone, is freed from any desire for material possessions by the simple fact that he thus has access to all possible joy. The desire for possessions represents typically what the Indian tradition calls a rebirth, the starting point of a new transient state. Anyone who wishes, say, to acquire a

---

30 The root *TAM* means first of all 'to run out of air', but the idea of darkness is also present and found in the word temerity, which properly means to make a move in the dark (from an old Latin word *temus*). According to the etymological dictionary of the Latin language by Ernout and Meillet, the word *tenebrae* also derives from the same root, despite the change of *m* to *n*. Of note is that the Vedic word *tamisrāḥ*, darkness, is always used in the plural, as it is in Latin.

more beautiful or powerful car than he already has, *de facto* creates a new mortal ego associated with this possession like a slave to his master. In other words, it gives birth to a new ephemeral enjoyer, whether the intention of the latter is particularly vile, as in the case of a rapist for example, or is of an elevated nature. The *Bhagavad-gītā* says in effect that even '*sattva* is bound by attachment to happiness and knowledge' (14, 6).[31] One should not forget that this *guṇa* is closely related to the other *guṇa* which can be easily illustrated in the following example: a beautiful piece of gold jewellery may be considered sattvic as an object, but it is often likely to generate a rajasic pride in those who possess it, and a tamasic desire in those who covet it. This is why this highest tendency must also be transcended, for it is only 'when the seer knows that which is beyond the *guṇa* that he attains to My being (*bhāva*)' (*ibid.*, 14, 19). That said, the *Bhāgavata-purāṇa* adds an interesting comment: 'One must overcome *tamas* and *rajas* with *sattva* and *sattva* with *sattva* itself' (11, 13, 1). Now, to free oneself from this kind of tyranny of the world is to acquire real peace of mind and, in this sense, Kṛṣṇa eminently deserves to be described as peaceful (*śanta*). In Christian terms: 'Seek ye first the kingdom of God, and his righteousness; and all these things [earthly goods] shall be added unto you' (Matthew 6:33).

Lastly, the Queen addresses Kṛṣṇa as Master of the monists (*kaivalya*). Here *bhakti* eminently merges with *jñāna-yoga*, the path of knowledge. The *kaivalya* is one

---

31 For example, Nicolas de Flue, leaving his wife and ten children and a thriving farm to become a hermit, renounced a purely sattvic happiness.

who considers God as unique (*kevala*) and who, in identifying with Him, realizes Him. In this way Kuntī creates a bridge between the Vaisnavite world, which is generally oriented towards *bhakti*, and the Śaivite world, which is more associated with the path of knowledge, where this term is commonly used: *Tadeko'vasiṣṭaḥ śivaḥ kevalo'ham*—'The One who remains, Śiva, the Unique, I am He' (Śaṅkara, *Daśaślokī*, 1). In an earlier passage, the *Bhāgavata-purāṇa* (1, 2, 11) states that those who know the truth call this one, namely the One God, either *brahman* (the Absolute) or *paramātman* (the Supreme Self) or *bhagavat* (the Lord). Swami Tapasyananda (1980: vol. 1, 7) sees in this an allusion to 'the Vedantins' (usually Śaivite), 'to the devotees of Hiraṇyagarbha (the golden embryo)' (that is to say of Brahmā, but we have seen in v. 1 that they have scarcely even a theoretical existence) and 'to the *bhakta*' (whose obedience is primarily Vaishnavite). Now, some of these *bhakta* Vaishnavites see this gradation: the first of the devotees mentioned by the *Bhāgavata-purāṇa* conceive of the One, the second see Him, and the third are grounded in Him. But this way of thinking has nothing specifically bhaktic, for one also finds it in Sufism which is typically jñānic. In his invaluable work, *The Book of Certainty* (1992: 12), Abū Bakr Sirāj al-Dīn describes a similar doctrine which has three levels that are made up of the Lore of Certainty (*ʿilm al-yaqīn*), the Eye of Certainty (*ʿayn al-yaqīn*) and the Truth of Certainty (*ḥaqq al-yaqīn*).

11. *I see in thee Time which reigns (over all things), without beginning or end, the Omnipresent, whose relentless onward*

march makes no distinction anywhere between his creatures, notwithstanding the conflicts that tear them apart.

Kṛṣṇa is here likened to Time, without beginning or end and who reigns (*īśāna*: this word derives from the same root indicating power as the word *īśvara*) over all things. He is also called *vibhu*, the Omnipresent, a word already encountered in v. 6, but which takes on a more specific meaning here due to its explicitly temporal context. The idea of a time without beginning and end seems to contradict the biblical verse proclaiming that 'In the beginning God created the Heavens and the Earth' and therefore, as some philosophers and theologians have deduced, also time. The idea of the eternity of the world, familiar to the Greeks and transmitted to the Latin West by the Arabs, provoked in the Western world a thorny controversy in the Middle Ages, leading to condemnations and dividing Christian thinkers (cf. Michon 2004).[32] But for India, as for the Stoics, it is obvious that the world is co-eternal with the Principle.[33] In other words, the latter suffers from incompleteness without its manifestation. As summarized by André Padoux,

> 'Indian theologies... whether they are Tantric or not, are emanationist, for nothing can be manifested in the world which is not there first in

32 The Islamic tradition experienced a similar debate. On the basis of a *ḥadīth*: 'Do not insult time (*dahr*), for God is time,' certain scholars, called the *al-dahriyya*, affirmed the eternity of the world and considered the word *dahr* a divine Name (Gimaret 1988: 186–7).

33 'Know that *prakṛti* and *puruṣa* are both without beginning' (*Bhagavad-gītā*, 13, 19).

> the divinity. In India there is no creation *ex nihilo*, no *fiat* after which everything is manifest: the creation is in a constant cyclical process flowing forth from the divinity and the link between manifestation and the divinity is continuous' (2010: 171 trans. DB).

The concept of the co-eternity of manifestation is also implicit in the figure of the serpent Śeṣa, who embodies this continuity from one cycle to another.

Manifestation, however, being only a sort of inward dimension of the Principle, is not identified with it. This is why the world is subject to becoming and must be destroyed and recreated periodically.[34] 'All beings, O son of Kuntī, are absorbed back into my *prakṛti* at the end of an era (*kalpa*). At the beginning of the next era I send them forth again' (*Bhagavad-gītā*, 9, 7). This is the metaphysical foundation of the doctrine of the four ages as well as the days and nights of Brahmā which is the subject of significant elaboration in Puranic literature. The two ways to solve the problem we have just described derive, philosophically, from a clash between a linear and a cyclical conception of time. We cannot stress enough

---

34 Guénon says, nevertheless: 'The world is not eternal because it is contingent, in other words, it has a beginning as well as an end, because it is not itself its own principle, or because it does not contain its principle in itself, that principle being necessarily transcendent with respect to it' (1945: 48). Obviously, he means in this case manifestation taken in isolation. It is only through its continuous recreation that the world participates in the eternity of the Principle. We can observe from all this that the controversy over the eternity of the world is largely a question of words and points of view.

the importance the choice of one or the other of these points of view makes on the collective imagination of a civilization. To consider an uninterrupted succession of creations and destructions allows one to conceive each cycle as a progressive degeneration without any 'pessimism', insofar as the order is re-established periodically. But when we consider a single creation, it becomes more difficult to conceive of a deteriorating spiritual humanity over time. Christians tend to see in the coming of Christ the beginning of an era of Grace which interrupted the process initiated by the fall of Adam, and thus they relegate the time before him to a sort of diffuse darkness, and this notwithstanding the warning signs that, according to the Gospel, must announce the end of time.[35] This way of seeing things is perhaps the origin of the theory of the continuous progress of mankind, as assumed by most historians, sociologists and scientists today. Whatever the value of its arguments, such an ideological position has psychological and spiritual consequences which are clearly disastrous, since modern man has a most unfortunate tendency to think himself better than his ancestors because he is 'more evolved' than them. Conversely, the Hindu considers himself, at least on the spiritual level, which is all that really matters to him, necessarily inferior to his predecessors of earlier ages.

The perception of time in India is something unique in the history of civilization. On the one hand, the *Purāṇa* cite astronomical figures in their descriptions of the various ages of the world. This is perhaps the only ex-

[35] The extremity of this attitude is reached when some theologians deny the possibility of entry into Heaven to all men born before Christ.

ample of a traditional calculation of time whose order of magnitude, if taken literally, is close to or exceeds the estimates of modern science. Such comparisons remain nevertheless fairly anecdotal. On the other hand, not only do Hindus often worry very little about their own age, but also, above all, they have almost never developed a historical consciousness like ours. We search in vain for figures like Thucydides or Livy in Sanskrit literature. In fact virtually all the dates of events in the history of India were established on the basis of comments made by foreign travellers, mainly Chinese, Arab or European. But on another level, Hindus are happy to glory in the age of their tradition, and Indian scholars do not hesitate to date the *Veda*, or at least the first of them, the *Ṛg-veda*, to an era going back four thousand years BC. Even if we reduce this to 1500 BC, which represents the average estimates of Western orientalists, the fact remains that the *sanātana-dharma* has very old roots. And let us not forget either that the *Veda* are made up of a corpus of texts consisting of over two thousand pages, which is a huge amount, and that in India, where almost nothing material has been preserved from this remote time, the only possible archaeology comes from philology.

Insofar as he embodies time, Kṛṣṇa is perfectly impartial (*sama*) in relation to creations like the sun which shines on all, or the rain that falls on both the fields of the just and the unjust. He is neither the enemy nor friend of anyone. However, there is a big 'but' in relation to this impartiality. In the *Bhagavad-gītā*, Kṛṣṇa says: 'I am the same to all beings, none of them is the object of my hatred, nor do I hold any dear (*priya*) to me. But those who worship me with devotion (*bhakti*) are in me and I am in them' (9, 29). Rāmakṛṣṇa glosses this verse: 'God is in all beings; but all beings are not in God. And that is the cause of their suffering.'[36]

At the end of the verse, it is implicitly with reference to this suffering that Kuntī alludes to the conflicts between men that tear them apart and cause them loss. The poet[37] employs here a paronomasia, a figure of speech which is extremely common in Sanskrit literature and which brings together two words that sound similar. *Kali*, conflict, thus combines with *kāla*, time.[38] Monier-Williams traces these two terms back to two roots that differ, but whose form is identical (*KAL*), and that in both cases have the same meaning: to emit a sound. *Kali* (probably close to calculation, calcium, or *caillou* in French, from the Latin *calx*) is the number one, the lowest throw of the dice. But following on from that, it also means conflict. *Kali-yuga* is also the age of conflicts.[39] While in the *Mahābhārata* it is Duryodhana who incarnates Kali, one may also note that in the *Bhāgavata-purāṇa* (4, 8, 3–4) Kali is also personified in a context independent of the epic. His father is Krodha

---

36 Quoted by Swami Chidbhavananda (1969: 517).

37 We do not really know how to designate the author of an anonymous work such as the *Bhāgavata-purāṇa*. He is both poet and prophet like the *vates* in Latin. Even the word author is ill-suited to a case like this, which refers *a priori* to divine inspiration. Tibullus, for example, said: *carminis auctor Apollo*, 'Apollo the author of my verses' (2, 4, 13).

38 The *kali-yuga* is sometimes called *kali-kāla*.

39 Although the *kali-yuga* is actually a dark age, this translation is probably due to a confusion between *kali* and *kāla* (see below).

(Anger) and his mother is Hiṃsā (Violence), and with his sister Durukti (Falsehood) he begets Bhaya and Mṛtyu, namely Fear and Death.

As for the term *kāla*, time (etymologically close to that of *calendae*, which in Rome were announced aloud by a priest at the beginning of each month and whose name gave rise to our calendar), it has a second meaning, that of darkness, and the feminine form of Kālī, the Black One, is one of the most famous names of the Goddess who is especially venerated in Calcutta (Kālikatā). The French phrase 'la nuit des temps' shows just how much these two notions agree to the point of being combined in a single idiom. But we have yet to conclude from the passage that we are commenting on that Kṛṣṇa, as a manifestation of time which destroys the world, has no interest in the conflicts between men: 'I am Time, which, in progressing, destroys the world. I am here, in this lower world, to destroy men. Even without you (Arjuna), all these soldiers arrayed to fight in the front line of battle, will not survive' (*Bhagavad-gītā*, 11, 32).

12. *O Lord, no one understands thy intentions in thy life here-below. Thou dost deceive men. No one is loved or hated by thee and yet in the minds of men thou dost seem partial.*

This verse seems to contradict Kṛṣṇa's assertion in the *Bhagavad-gītā* that: 'I am born from age to age to protect the good, destroy the wicked and reaffirm *dharma*' (4, 8). But here it refers to the mysterious aspect of God's action in the world that we have already discussed in the dice game, v. 7. The paradox here is that this obscure dimension of the divinity is reflected in the existence of the avatar. Voltaire and others have argued in a well-known formula that if God created man in his own image, man has more than returned the compliment.[40] Although this statement contains some truth *sui generis*, it takes very little account of everything in the behaviour of the avatar that defies common sense. Why would man create a God who disturbs him? The early followers of Christ were greatly troubled by his message before realizing that the Kingdom promised by their Master was not an earthly one, and the Jews were shocked to see him pick the ears of corn on the Sabbath. The heroes of the epic are thus faced with a number of inexplicable actions on the part of Kṛṣṇa. We will consider only two of them here, both of which have in common a shocking and immoral outward appearance, as they clearly break the law imposed on men.

The first of these behaviours involves the relations that the adolescent Kṛṣṇa has with the gopis, the milkmaids of Vṛndāvana wood. Tradition tells us that all these young women, including Rādhā,[41] the favourite

40 Voltaire is not the first one to have observed this: 'Men imagine the gods to be born, and to have clothes, and voices and shapes like theirs... Yea, the gods of the Ethiopians are black and flat-nosed, the gods of the Thracians are red-haired and blue-eyed... Yea, if oxen, horses and lions had hands and could shape with their hands images as do men, horses would fashion their gods as horses, and oxen as oxen...' But it is here a question of the gods with a lower case 'g', and the same author quotes further on: 'There is one God... neither in shape nor thought like unto mortals... He abideth ever in the same place motionless ... and without effort swayeth all things by his force of mind' (Xenophanes of Colophon, 6th century BC, quoted by Koestler, *The Sleepwalkers*, 1959, p. 24).

41 In fact, Rādhā is not part of the *Mahābhārata* or the

lover of the god, were indeed already married, and that these relations were actually adulterous. Similarly, much later in his life, when Kṛṣṇa, then King of Dvārakā, delivered the sixteen thousand women prisoners from the demon Bhaumāsura, these women refused to return to the homes of their husbands. He then united with them simultaneously in sixteen thousand palaces that he had made for them. Certainly, in India no devotee sees in this an invitation to any sort of lustful behaviour.[42] But the epic relates that some of the avatar's contemporaries were offended by this freedom, starting with Rādhā herself, who at first refused him, and Nārada, the Vedic sage who on visiting Kṛṣṇa asked him to explain himself. These reactions forced the hand of the exegetes, making them go beyond the level of social exemplarism and see in these events only their symbolic meaning, namely a mystical image of the soul's relationship with God. To unite with the deity, our soul must commit adultery and deceive, so to speak, the world. Coomaraswamy (1985: 104) summarizes it thus: 'Here illicit love becomes the very type of salvation: for in India where social convention is so strict, such a love involves the surrender of all that the world values and sometimes of life itself.' The medieval exegetes of the Bible, starting with Ambrose of

---

Bhāgavata-purāṇa. It was Jayadeva who was the first to popularise this essential Krishnaite figure in his famous *Gīta-Govinda* (late 12th century). It is in this context that we can consider her part of the epic in the broader meaning we have given this term (cf. ch. 1).

42 André Padoux (2010: 159–160) mentions some Tantric sexual rites inspired by the relationship between Rādhā and Kṛṣṇa, but it is not a question of lust in this case.

Milan in his *Apology of David*, have also not interpreted otherwise the adultery of David and Bathsheba, Uriah personifying then the profane world. The fact, not always obvious to pious readers, that the literalness of Scripture must, in some cases, be rejected or surpassed, is an important lesson of the Fathers of the Church. Generally cited in support of this exegetical position are the verses in the Gospel which require one to be a eunuch to enter the Kingdom of Heaven or to hate one's father and mother. Similarly, in the Old Testament, a literal interpretation of the duration of the world leads to a narrow and pernicious creationism. Lastly, after asking Abraham to sacrifice what he holds most dear, namely his son, God makes it clear to the patriarch, after testing his resolve, that he must fulfil his intention by making an offering that is symbolic and not strictly literal.

The second of these problematic behaviours are the multiple ruses that Kṛṣṇa advises his comrades in arms to use in the battle of Kurukṣetra. It would take too long to list them all, and we will take only two as examples. The Pāṇḍava are faced with the impossibility of defeating Droṇa, their old master of arms, who has remained faithful, despite himself, to the Kaurava clan. Kṛṣṇa asks the Pāṇḍava to falsely declare that Aśvatthāman, Droṇa's son, has died in battle. But initially Droṇa does not believe them and he demands that Yudhiṣṭhira himself, who is known for never having told a lie, confirm this. But the eldest Pāṇḍava cannot bring himself to use this stratagem. To help him overcome this scruple, an elephant with the same name as Droṇa's son is killed. Then, very reluctantly, Yudhiṣṭhira proclaims to his opponent that 'Aśvatthāman, the elephant, is dead,' pronouncing the word elephant so quietly that Droṇa cannot hear it. Droṇa, thus misled, is so thrown by this that he lets himself be killed without putting up a fight. Given that the intention was to deceive, and in spite of the extenuating ruse of the Pāṇḍava, this constituted a full-blown lie and not merely, as circumstances would make appear, a 'half lie', which is a rather meaningless expression anyway. What is more, it is the son of Dharma, the epitome of righteousness, who speaks thus, and to none other than his own guru! It is said that Yudhiṣṭhira, who previously rode in his war chariot hovering slightly above the ground, suddenly went down a notch, and the wheels of his vehicle began to squeak and raise up clouds of dust.

In discussing the question of the vow of truth that all yogis must abide by, Tara Michaël (1980: 83) cites several passages from the *Mahābhārata* justifying this type of lie. Bhīṣma, for example, says: 'Rather than the literal truth, we must say what will lead to the greater good for all, because what is the greatest good for all, in my opinion, is the real truth' (12, 109, 15–16). So what one must remember, according to Vyāsa, the author of the main commentary on the *Yoga-sūtra*, and not the author of the *Mahābhārata*, is that 'the truth should never be uttered if the result will be to inflict an evil on creatures, but only if it is for a beneficial purpose' (*ibid*). Similarly in *Aethiopica* (26), Heliodorus names two conditions when it is permissible to lie. It must be helpful for the one that says it but it must not harm the one who hears it.

Later, towards the end of the battle, when Duryodhana and Bhīma are facing each other in single combat wielding clubs, Kṛṣṇa tells Bhīma, who is in very real danger from his opponent, that he should strike him on the thigh, contrary to all the rules of combat between *kṣatriya* knights. The person who is the most taken aback by this forbidden behaviour is curiously enough Duryodhana himself, the embodiment of Kali, the brother and husband of Durukti (Falsehood; cf. ch. 11). But no doubt he realizes that he has been punished in this manner at the very place on his body where he himself had sinned. For at the end of the dice game, once he has seized Draupadī and made it clear that he will have her, he strikes his thigh with his hand in front of the Pāṇḍava to signify that their wife in common now belongs to him. The Vaisnavite exegesis concludes that adharmic (*adharmika*) behaviour such as Kṛṣṇa's is justified, especially in the *kali-yuga*, to the extent that it seeks to restore a higher *dharma*. Nevertheless, we have heard it said that some Hindus in our time still have a struggle accepting this character trait of Kṛṣṇa.

In the Greek world, a mission similar to that of Kṛṣṇa's is taken on by Ulysses whose deceptions also serve a legitimate cause, namely the recovery of Helen, the adulterous wife of Menelaus, who has been unjustly abducted by Paris. Although Homer portrays Ulysses as a 'positive' hero, Virgil in the *Aeneid* takes the side of the Trojans, seeing in Ulysses and the Greeks the prototypes of a humanity perverting the use of the intelligence. His *timeo Danaos* is like a nostalgia for a purer mind, that of the men of the Bronze Age exalted by the Romans in all their literature, with its ideal of the citizen-soldier who is courageous, sober and hardworking. The Latin Middle Ages also inherited distrust for this form of intelligence, and the Church would always fear men who 'think', but here is how Titus Burckhardt restores the character of Ulysses to its rightful place:

> 'The fact that Ulysses is the *protégé* of Pallas Athena, the goddess of wisdom, forces us to believe that the guile he shows on almost every occasion and which is almost his most salient characteristic, did not, in the spiritual cosmos of the ancient Greeks play the same negative role as it did for a Christian like Dante, who places Ulysses in one of the most terrible regions of hell, as a liar and deceiver *par excellence*. For the Greeks, Ulysses's guile amounted to a capacity to dissimulate and persuade which in itself was positive; it was the sign of a sovereign intelligence and almost a magic of the spirit that could penetrate and fathom other's thoughts' (1987: 159–160).

As regards the Bible, Abraham similarly asks his wife to lie to Pharaoh, and later he lies himself to Gerar (Genesis 12: 10ff., and 20: 2). Other patriarchs also had recourse to this kind of guile in various circumstances, but it is Jacob above all, especially when he 'steals' the birthright of his brother, who legitimizes deception in the biblical tradition. In addition to the abolition of the human sacrifice originally demanded of Abraham, the appearance of deception in sacred history seems to mark a transition comparable to that of entry into the *kali-yuga*.[43]

---

[43] In his *De mendacio* Augustine almost completely condemns the use of lying, and more than one Christian martyr died because of it. Eventually the Church had to water down its

In Islam, the Prophet did but confirm this state of affairs associated with the degeneration that comes with time. When he sent Nu'aym against the besiegers of Medina during the Battle of the Trench, he said: 'Do your best to sow enmity between them!' And when Nu'aym asked if he was allowed to lie, the Prophet replied: 'Say what thou wilt to draw them off us; for war is deception!' (Lings 1983: 225).

13. *O Soul of the universe, thy birth and thy action among the beasts, men, sages and sea monsters is ever a mystery, O thou who art non-born and non-acting.*

Kṛṣṇa is here called Soul (or Self) of the universe (*viśvātman*), the root VIŚ signifying total penetration, from which comes the meaning of the word 'all' for the adjective *viśva*. The translation of this by the word 'universe' is quite opportune since *universum* is 'the totality of things turned towards one (goal)', or perhaps better, 'that which is turned towards the one'. Although the *Bhāgavata-purāṇa* can be considered a text deeply rooted in the tradition of Vaishnavite *bhakti*, it remains, just like Hinduism in general, pervaded by its Vedic inheritance, which is always an underlying presence, like harmonics constantly heard and reinterpreted (see Introduction). This scenario is in fact little different from the relationship between Christianity and Judaism, the former not abolishing the latter, but fulfilling it via a new perspective. Thus, it is perhaps not without relevance to

---

wine: 'While lying is intrinsically evil, it is lawful if the duty to tell the truth is in conflict with another duty of a higher order' (A. Boulenger, *La Doctrine catholique*, Paris, 1936, vol. 2, p. 145). This is called a white lie.

mention here that Viśvā is a Vedic deity considered to be the mother of a dozen gods, the *viśve-deva*, 'all the gods', 'the gods taken as a whole', and no doubt for the devotee of Kṛṣṇa, the avatar manifests within himself this totality. However, in the context of *bhakti*, it is even worth asserting that this multitude of gods clearly refers to all creatures, composed of the different elements that God penetrates and vivifies (see Coomaraswamy, 1971: 14). In any case, from a theological point of view, *bhakti* is undeniably a simplification of the Vedic tradition, *ad maiorem Dei gloriam*.

The translation of the word *ātman* by 'soul' is, in contrast, more problematic, because of the vagueness surrounding this word in Western philosophy and theology, not to mention current usage. In fact, according to etymology, the *ātman* is the breath, the breath of life that animates all beings. It is also the primary meaning of the Latin words *animus* and *anima*, from which the French word *âme* is derived. One could also say that Kṛṣṇa is the spirit of the universe, because *spiritus* is also a name for the vital breath. As for the variant: 'O Self of the universe', though less elegant poetically speaking, it is justified both metaphysically and because the word *ātman* is the reflexive pronoun in Sanskrit.[44] Thus *jīvātman*, the living individual, is illusorily separate from *paramātman*, the Supreme Being. This truth is eminently

44 This is also often the case with the words *spiritus, anima* or *corpus* in Latin. French has kept this meaning in the expression *à son corps défendant* (against one's will), where there is no question of the body itself. The German verb *atmen*, breathe, also comes from the same root as *ātman*, like the Greek word *atmos*, found in the word atmosphere, i.e. breathable space.

expressed by one of the most cited *mahāvākya*, or great Upanisadic formulas: *ayamātmā brahma* 'this *ātman* is *brahman*, this Self is the Absolute' (*Māṇḍūkyopaniṣad*, 2). This is the supreme identity that nevertheless cannot be realized by just anyone. It is only offered as a grace to the one who has literally 'discovered' the *ātman* within himself, or rather he in whom the *ātman* has discovered its own Self: 'This *ātman* cannot be achieved by doctrine (only), the intelligence (alone) or numerous teachings. It is the *ātman* who chooses who attains it, he in whom the *ātman* has discovered its own Self' (*Muṇḍakopaniṣad*, 3, 2, 3).

The Sanskrit word translated by 'mystery' in this verse, *viḍambana*, is the same as the one in the previous verse that we have rendered by the idea of deception. If the general intention of the divinity seems clear in his incarnation, namely to make the world a means of salvation and not of perdition for men, we can still say that two things remain ever (*atyanta*) mysterious. On the one hand, the ability of God to incarnate—this birth of the non-born[45] and this act of non-acting—goes beyond reason and remains paradoxical to it. Christians rightly speak of the mystery of the Incarnation. If Jesus moves in a historical and not mythical world like Kṛṣṇa, he nevertheless ruptures in his way the order of things, the laws of the world, with his many miracles, starting with his virgin birth. The miracle trumps reason, and the man who does not believe it with his eyes must believe it in his

45 Thus Kṛṣṇa designates himself in the *Bhagavad-gītā* (4, 6). The birth of the non-born is sometimes compared to the sun that seems to be born each morning, although it has been there forever.

heart. On the other hand, the avatar is just as mysterious when one considers his different ways of behaving, even in what appear in him as limitations. Why, if he is all-powerful, must Kṛṣṇa be born after his six older brothers have been horribly murdered? Why does he not simply destroy the Kaurava army without further ado? And so on...[46] These questions form the starting point of the path for a *bhakta* and not for a *jñānin*. They demand absolute trust, and a blind faith in the message of Kṛṣṇa. 'The man who meditates on the mysterious birth of the Lord and invokes him in the morning and evening is delivered from the miseries of the world' (*Bhāgavata-purāṇa*, 1, 3, 29).

Kuntī also mentions that the avatar is born among beasts, men, sages (*ṛṣi*) and sea monsters. This refers to the multiple incarnations of Viṣṇu which are deemed to be as countless as the waves of the sea, the sea that is *brahman*, but concerning which the *Bhāgavata-purāṇa* (1, 3, 6–25) provides a limited list of twenty-two incarnations. This includes, in addition to the wild boar, fish and turtle, a number of *ṛṣi*, like Nārada, who appears in several different epochs, or Nara and Nārāyaṇa, the latter two being an inseparable pair who are found in the *Mahābhārata* in the form of the two heroes, Arjuna and Kṛṣṇa, respectively.[47] Some have thought they saw in the list of the ten most famous major incarnations

---

46 Likewise the soldiers to Jesus on the cross: 'If thou be the king of the Jews, save thyself!' (Luke 23:37).

47 This pair is reminiscent of the Dioscuri, the twins of Leda, the one, Pollux, son of Zeus, and the other Castor, son of Tyndareus; the first of divine origin, the second with a human father.

of Viṣṇu, with their passage from fish to tortoise, then boar, man-lion, dwarf and finally to actual human figures like Rāma with an axe, Rāmacandra, Kṛṣṇa, Buddha and Kalki, a quasi-Darwinian progression. But beyond the fact that Kalki at the end of the list is usually depicted with a horse's head, and that this order is far from being common to all the *Purāṇa*, this interpretation raises yet other problems. For example, as the boar, Viṣṇu saves the earth itself (the physical plane), as the tortoise he saves the means of terrestrial enjoyment (the vital plane), and as the fish he saves man as such (the mental plane).[48] Moreover, it is in this resolutely anti-evolutionary order and with several intercalations that these three incarnations appear in the *Bhāgavata-purāṇa* which then lists them differently in the history of the four ages.

14. *When thou didst commit mischief, the milkmaid (Yaśodā) immediately took a rope (to tie thee to a mortar). Thine eyes filled with tears and thy collyrium became smudged. Troubled by apprehension thou didst lower thy head. I was amazed for Fear itself fears thee.*

The episode recounted here took place during Kṛṣṇa's childhood. The latter, with his half-brother Balarāma, used to steal butter from the neighbouring houses. The two rascals guzzled it down or gave it to their playmates, or to the monkeys and other animals. Although full of affection for these urchins, the villagers complained constantly about them to their mothers, Rohinī and Yaśodā. One day Kṛṣṇa even broke a jar in his

48 We follow here an interpretation recounted by Jean Herbert, [1947] 1972: 321–2.

own house, and having had enough of this, his adoptive mother tied him to a heavy mortar by means of a rope wrapped round his belly. It is in reference to this event that he became known as Dāmodara, 'He who has a rope around the belly.' His tears smudged the collyrium which both adorned and protected his eyes. Thereafter the naughty child attempted to get rid of the heavy mortar in a spectacular fashion. Pulling it behind him he crawled on all fours between two huge acacia trees to jam it and tear the rope in two. But he only succeeded in uprooting the trees!

Several aspects of this adventure need to be considered. We have already explained above (v. 4) the symbolic meaning of the adoption of the avatar who somehow has to be welcomed and accepted by the world. We would like to explore this idea further by highlighting a strange parallel between the figure of Kṛṣṇa and his cousin Karṇa. Both had a miraculous birth. Having been delivered of her eldest child, the son of Sūrya, Kuntī, as we have seen, regained her virginity. In turn, Devakī, who was certainly not a virgin after six deliveries and the transfer of her seventh embryo to the womb of her co-wife, was nevertheless delivered of her eighth child contrary to the laws of nature and without pain. For according to the *Bhāgavata-purāṇa*, in the middle of that fateful night, Viṣṇu appeared to her in his majestic form with four arms and was transformed at once into a baby in her arms. Then these two new-born babies were immediately, for various reasons, abandoned by their mothers. It is said in the case of Karṇa that, being the son of the Sun, like the latter he had two mothers, namely the Night and the Dawn.[49] But the comparison does not stop there. At the time of their transfer to their adoptive parents, both divine offspring had to undergo a kind of baptism by water. While Karṇa was consigned to a river like Moses, Kṛṣṇa was put in a basket by his father Vasudeva, who placed him on his head to cross the Yamunā, symbolizing, in this case, *saṃsāra*, the flow of transient existence, in order to take him to Nanda and Yaśodā. The river, usually calm, suddenly unleashed its waves, which tried to lick the feet of the new-born babe, as if the whole world aspired to receive his blessing. Everything happened as if the avatar, in a first movement, descended vertically and timelessly in the darkness of the world into matter (from the Latin *mater*!). Then, it was only in a second movement that he seemed to enter horizontally into time and to be received into the world. It was only once Kṛṣṇa was adopted, as the dawn broke, that his life, like after a second birth, began in the full light of day within the history of men.[50] The similarity between the two cousins also manifests itself in the fact that they became the two most famous charioteers in the epic, the first voluntarily assuming this task for Arjuna, the second because he was found by Adhiratha and Rādhā,[51] who were members of this caste. It is therefore curious that Arjuna was both

49 See Dumézil 1986[5]: 129.

50 The life of Jesus, who had only one mother, is divided into two in a different way, namely the thirty years of his hidden life and then his public life that lasted three years. Or again, he was born of the Virgin Mary, but was adopted by Joseph.

51 This is of course another Rādhā than the one in the *Gīta-Govinda*.

the intimate friend of one and the personal enemy of the other.

To return to the incident of the butter, what is most striking about this is the perfect submission the divine child shows to his adoptive mother, who, the text suggests, also did not realize who her son really was, at least not until she had to clean his open mouth (cf. v. 1). She was barely able to find enough pieces of rope to tie the child up with, and was ridiculed by the gopis, her neighbours, before Kṛṣṇa agreed to let her attach him, out of compassion for his mother (*Bhāgavata-purāṇa*, 10, 9). But 'spare the rod and spoil the child,' and for the Krishnaites, Yaśodā's attitude is one of the five fundamental modes or flavours (*rasa*) of devotional love, in expressing as it does the feelings of parental love (*vātsalya-rasa*), of which Kuntī, as the avatar's aunt, is also a great example. The four other modes of these paths are that of the devotee who dedicates himself totally to the deity like a slave (*dāsya-rasa*), the peaceful way of the one who humbles himself before the divinity (*śānti-rasa*), the way of friendship (*sākhya-rasa*), modelled on the attitude of the young cow herders, and finally the 'honeyed' way (*mādhurya-rasa*), which magnifies the feelings of amorous love exemplified by the gopis.[52] It may be noted that the people who seem to have any real 'power' over Kṛṣṇa, are, like his adoptive mother Yaśodā and his lover Rādhā, only able to obtain this prerogative by showing total and perfect love.

The episode of the jar of butter reveals yet another aspect of Kṛṣṇa as the transgressor, which is also an

---

52 See Sailley (1986: 145ff.).

enigma to his contemporaries since his opponents at Kurukṣetra reproach him for it; and, indeed, before stealing women, Kṛṣṇa was also a butter thief. He thus takes for himself the quintessential pleasures of the world. Selfishness being by definition alien to the spirit of the avatar, there thus remains only a mystical or esoteric interpretation which can account for this difficulty. In fact, Kṛṣṇa is the exclusive enjoyer (*bhoktṛ*) of the world, as of all sacrificial acts (cf. *Bhagavad-gītā*, 5, 29). To realize this is to realize *brahman*: 'When you have understood who the enjoyer, the object of enjoyment and the inciter is (the supreme god), you have understood all. This is the triple *brahman*' (*Śvetāśvataropaniṣad*, 1, 12).[53] Ultimately, it is Kṛṣṇa who enjoys everything in us which we imagine in our illusion that we are enjoying ourselves.

The most touching aspect in the story of Dāmodara is that the child who cries is he whom Fear itself fears. This is the only time, to our knowledge, when Kṛṣṇa shows a human[54] weakness, as if, at least once in his life on some level, he had to show by doing this that he had become a man like any other. Whereas Jesus, the man, sweats blood and tears in the Garden of Olives and cries out: 'Father, all things are possible unto thee; take away this cup from me!' (Mark 14:36), Kṛṣṇa passes through all

---

53 In this very ancient *Upaniṣad* a sort of trinity of *brahman*, which develops in its own way the equation *ātman* = *brahman*, appears for the first time.

54 This 'weakness' is also relative. For a crying child inspires tenderness which entails the parental feeling we have just spoken of. We also acknowledge that Kṛṣṇa is the victim of an all too human weakness when, believing that Rādhā has rejected him, he falls into a terrible lovelorn despair.

the tribulations of the world with perfect immunity, as if floating on a cloud. He is clearly distinct from Rāma who has to undergo the abduction of his wife and then later divorce her because of other men's spite. For some, including many Christians specifically, this privilege seems almost 'inappropriate', as if it distances the avatar from ordinary people by sparing him all their trials. But the Krishnaite path of renunciation is more happy than austere, 'its burden is light.' That is why Kṛṣṇa is represented most of the time in the iconography with an indefinable smile on his face, as equally mysterious and famous as the Mona Lisa's, except that his is charming.[55] He is never without it, and as stated in the text, especially not when he is about to kill an enemy, such as Kaṃsa or Śiśupāla. From his childhood onwards, he always seems to handle difficulties with ease. When he tames Kāliya, the demon with the body of a snake and many heads who is terrorising the villagers, he does it as if it were a game, and he ends up dancing on its head. A constant trait in his behaviour is that he always seems to intervene in an effortless manner, even when he lifts up a mountain like a sort of umbrella to protect an entire village from the deluge of Indra. His love of fun results in still other episodes, such as when he hides the gopis' clothes when they are bathing in the river, so that they are forced to come out naked. Kṛṣṇa is a joker god. Let us include, however, the esoteric meaning that Frithjof Schuon gives this episode: 'The theft of the saris

55 The Mona Lisa, for her part, seems to have a forced smile which gives credence to the hypothesis that her smile imitates Sarah's, who at almost a hundred, laughed in disbelief at the announcement of her pregnancy with Isaac.

symbolizes the loss of individuality in the love of God, then its restitution on a higher plane, that of detachment; but it may also symbolize, in a more general fashion, the divine requirement that the soul should appear naked in front of its Creator' (1981: 58).

It will be a question now of seeing how the other characters in the epic interpret Kṛṣṇa's mission in the following four verses.

15. *Some say that thou, the non-born, were born in the lineage of the beloved Yadu to the glory of this man of good reputation (Yudhiṣṭhira?) as sandalwood is to the glory of the mountains of Malaya.*

To begin with, this verse contains a problem of interpretation on which we must pause. Swami Tapasyananda understands the man of good reputation in question to be none other than Yadu himself, the distant ancestor of Kṛṣṇa who, after having been disinherited by his father, became the magnanimous king of the Mathurā region (cf. ch. 1). This monarch deserves the epithet beloved in the text here, probably because he was appreciated both by his subjects and by Indra who generously saved him from a flood. But 'man of good reputation' (*puṇya-śloka*, 'He who is spoken well of') is either a common name referring to Yadu or one of the proper names given in the epic to Yudhiṣṭhira, the son of Kuntī, who, we must remember, is present at this scene and could very easily be pointed out by the Queen to her interlocutor.[56] In fact this is the solution we prefer in the light of the prin-

56 Swami Prabhupāda extricates himself by making Kuntī say in substance 'some claim you were born for the glory of Yadu and others for that of Yudhiṣṭhira.'

ciple of *lectio difficilior*. Moreover, it can be argued that the avatar is necessarily born in order to meet a need. What need is there to enhance the glory of Yadu, long-gone centuries past? In contrast, the Kurukṣetra War is an emergency imperatively calling for divine intervention. Now, we know that in this conflict Kṛṣṇa ultimately decides in favour of Yudhiṣṭhira, and the circumstances surrounding this decision deserve to be examined.

Firstly, the legitimate claims of the eldest Pāṇḍava should be noted. His father, Pāṇḍu, was crowned first because, although his half-brother, Dhṛtarāṣṭra, was first in line of succession to Śāntanu, he was blind. Then he himself was born before his cousin Duryodhana, to the chagrin of the latter's parents, since Duryodhana's mother Gāndhārī, although pregnant before Kuntī, had to endure a two-year pregnancy before giving birth to an iron ball[57] that was divided into a hundred pieces and put in pots, then allowed to 'hatch' into her one hundred sons. Finally, due to his character, which was imbued with nobility and respect for *dharma*, Yudhiṣṭhira was widely acclaimed king, in contrast to the scheming Duryodhana. It was he, moreover, that Dhṛtarāṣṭra initially appointed as heir to the throne, preferring him, against all expectations, to his own son. But although Kṛṣṇa was closer in kin to the Pāṇḍava than the Kaurava, being the nephew of Kuntī, he long remained neutral in the dynastic debate. It was only after the infamous game of dice, the exile of the Pāṇḍava and their wife, and the

---

57 The mention of iron is incidentally brought in here in connection with the *kali-yuga*, in the absence of a systematic reference to metals in relation to the four ages, as in the Greek tradition.

subsequent refusal of Duryodhana to return their part of the kingdom to them, which he had promised to do after their exile, that Kṛṣṇa, after various attempts at mediation, chose in the end to support the Pāṇḍava clan. In addition, in appearance at least, it was not he who chose whose side he was on. Indeed, when the war became inevitable, Duryodhana and Arjuna had the same idea and went to him to win his allegiance. With his customary arrogance, Duryodhana arrived first, found Kṛṣṇa asleep, and immediately went and stood by his head, hoping, through this manoeuvre, to be the first to talk to him when he woke up and thus win his favour. But 'the last shall be first,' and when Kṛṣṇa opened his eyes, he saw Arjuna directly in front of him first; for in deference to the avatar the Pāṇḍava had remained at his feet, with palms together waiting for him to wake up. It was therefore to him that Kṛṣṇa made his famous offer: he declared himself ready to yield his considerable army to one of the rival clans, while making available to the other his exclusive person, but only on condition that he not be required to fight. 'Give up all your duties (*dharma*), take me as your sole refuge. I will free you from all your troubles, do not worry' (*Bhagavad-gītā*, 16, 66). Arjuna did not hesitate a moment. He chose the avatar, leaving the army to Duryodhana, who was overcome with joy at the prospect of such a windfall. Assuredly, he who is called the great archer, Arjuna, preferred at this critical moment the inner spiritual power of the 'non-acting' one, his true *śakti*, over his possible power over the things of this world, leaving his misguided cousin the victim of an ephemeral illusion in taking the shadow for reality.

To return to the opinion mentioned by Kuntī of those

who saw in the birth of the non-born a providential intervention in favour of Yudhiṣṭhira, it can be said that they were not wrong. Indeed, Kṛṣṇa himself gives three reasons for his successive appearances: 'From age to age I manifest in order to strengthen *dharma*, to protect the good (*sādhu*) and destroy the wicked' (*Bhagavad-gītā*, 4, 8). Now, this necessary function through the ages, in other words beyond the 'physical' presence of the avatar, is ultimately the sacred duty of all legitimate kings. Kṛṣṇa, at the dawn of the fourth age, could not, in practice, act otherwise than in promoting the succession of a temporal sovereign who was a guarantor of peace for humanity.[58] We are here in the realm of nature, in the domain of the *guṇa*. This is why the *Sāṃkhya* (*Sāṃkhyakārikā*, 12) specifies that the duty of upholding the law, as confided to a king, is in itself a rajasic act. However, due to the interplay of forces that govern the universe, this function has a sattvic effect in protecting the good and a tamasic effect in the punishment of the wicked. The etymologist will further argue that the words *rajas* and *rājan* (king) derive from related roots.

16. *Others believe that thou didst come into the world in answer to the prayer of Vasudeva and Devakī. Thou art the non-born come to establish peace on earth and kill those who hate the gods.*

At first glance this verse seems to have the same meaning as the preceding one, but it extends the cause of the avatar's coming further back in time. It is said

---

[58] In his lifetime Jesus only cared for the Kingdom of Heaven that is 'within you'. But afterwards the Christians had to entrust their kings with a sacred mission.

that Vasudeva and Devakī were King Sutapas and Queen Pṛśni in a previous life, and that they underwent great austerities in order to have a child. The name Sutapas actually means 'He who performs great asceticism.' It is in fact impossible to count the number of characters in Indian mythology who have acquired merit through severe austerities. This practice is related to the doctrine of *karman*, which means that any action necessarily bears a fruit. Thus asceticism, *tapas*, literally 'heat', gives men and demons a real power over the gods who are forced to honour the merits earned in this way, whether the intention of the ascetic be good or bad. Sutapas and Pṛśni's intention was certainly pure, because when Kṛṣṇa appeared to reward them, they asked him for a son 'like you'. Their perfect devotion to the One, the non-born, could only compel the deity to incarnate himself. The royal couple were then reborn on earth to see their wish fulfilled. But as we have seen, the privilege of giving birth to an avatar exacts a very high price, as if the powers of darkness rebel one last time to prevent such an arrival: *Semperque magno constitit nasci deum*, 'The birth of a god always comes at great cost,' says Seneca (*Hercules furens*, 462).

What has changed in this verse, in contrast to the previous one, is the use of a new verb to describe the coming of the avatar. It is not said that the non-born is 'born', but that he literally 'approached' (*abhyagāt*), which we have taken into account in saying he has 'come into the world'. But in a more literal sense, one could say that in coming into the world he came close, he became the neighbour, above all of Vasudeva and Devakī, and subsequently of all men. In the famous parable of the good Samaritan (Luke 10: 28–37), a lawyer, referring to the commandment: 'Thou shalt love thy neighbour as thyself' (cf. Lev. 19: 18), asks Jesus who is the neighbour? However, against all expectations, Jesus does not say it is the man attacked by robbers who was the neighbour who should be loved as ourselves and therefore rescued. Instead he directs his interlocutor, and us at the same time, to put ourselves in the place of the unfortunate beaten man left half dead on the road. Then he asks the questioner: 'Which now, of these three, thinkest thou, was neighbour unto him that fell among the thieves?' And the man answers correctly that it is the one who showed mercy to the victim. Thus the neighbour to the man in distress, our neighbour, is neither the priest nor the Levite who passes by. The one that we need to love as ourselves is not so and so with all his imperfections, but He who is within all beings, He who manifests in order to help us, namely the avatar. The Good Samaritan is an image of Christ who leans towards human suffering in this vale of tears which is the world. He it is who in reality is the neighbour who is to be loved 'with an undivided mind occupied by nothing else (*ananyamanas*)' as in the passage from the *Bhagavad-gītā* that we mentioned in the Introduction. In the Islamic tradition, God is also presented as near to man, especially in this well-known verse: 'We (God) are nearer to him (man) than his jugular vein' (Qur'ān 50: 16). And for the Sufi Ibn 'Aṭā' Allāh (d. 1309), it is precisely because of this proximity that we have difficulty in contemplating God: 'Only His extreme nearness to you is what veils God from you, only because of the intensity of His manifestation is He veiled and only because of the sublimity of His Light is He hidden from view' (H. 164–165, Danner, 1978: 88). Several divine Names evoke this same reality: *al-Qarīb*, the Near; *al-Walī*, the Most Near; *al-Wālī*, the very close Master, at least if one translates these last two terms according to etymology, as does Gloton (2002: 850).

In a famous passage of the *Bṛhadāraṇyakopaniṣad* the sage Yājñavalkya says: 'Verily, it is not for the love of the husband that the husband is dear. It is for the sake of the *ātman* (or "self" or, better still, "the Self") that the husband is dear. It is not for the love of the wife that the wife is dear. It is for the sake of the *ātman* that the wife is dear. It is not for the love of the son that the son is dear. It is for the sake of the *ātman* that the son is dear' (4, 5, 6). The list continues and extends to the riches of this world, to *brahman*, power, worlds, gods, creatures and the All. Yājñavalkya concludes: 'In truth, it is the *ātman* one must see and hear, must think about and meditate on. All this, O Maitreyī,[59] is known through the vision, hearing, thinking and discernment of the *ātman*.'

We can conclude by saying that the commandment: 'Thou shalt love thy neighbour as thyself' allows us, obviously, to love ourselves. But we still need to know who we are. It is certainly not the petty ego which is to be loved, but the *ātman* which is in us and which is embodied by Kṛṣṇa: 'I live in the heart of all beings' (*Bhagavad-gītā*, 15, 15). To identify this reality is to know oneself in the sense of the aphorism of Delphi. This is the supreme identity which makes God our only neighbour, intimate friend, and *alter ego*. Thus Coomaraswamy says:

---

59 Note that Yājñavalkya is addressing his speech to a female disciple.

'It is this Self that the man who really loves himself or others, loves in himself and in them' (1971: 13).

The end of this verse in the queen's speech seems to gloss the passage of the *Bhagavad-gītā* (4, 8) cited concerning the previous verse, where the protection of the good and punishment of the wicked is mentioned. Only the words have changed. For it is a question specifically here of establishing peace or security (*kṣema*), and refers not to those who do evil, but to people who hate the celestial beings (*sura*). This last word has a curious origin. It comes from the word *asura*, which is neutral in itself, meaning a spirit, a subtle being; but with time it has taken on a negative meaning, like the word demon in the Western tradition. In usage the initial *a* of *asura* has thus been assimilated to a privative *a*, which it is not, and so the word *sura* was invented, as if it were a cognate of *svar*, the sky. At any rate, the descent of the avatar is always a crisis in the strongest sense of the word, that is to say, a judgement. It forces men to reveal their fundamental nature and for some, therefore, a real hatred of the supernatural and the transcendent. Rewarding the good and punishing the wicked, the avatar exercises, in Islamic terms, what is called Mercy and Rigour or Wrath (*al-raḥmah wa 'l-ghaḍab*), corresponding to the two hands of God. The emblems of Viṣṇu are sometimes interpreted in this way: he has two destructive weapons, the disc and the mace, and two attributes which spread his blessings, the conch and the lotus.

17. *Still others believe that thou wert born at the request of Brahmā to alleviate the burden of the world, like a ship sinking due to an excessive load.*

This new way of seeing things is based on the well-known relationship between the three gods of the Hindu *trimūrti*: Brahmā, who assumes the creative function, Viṣṇu, who preserves the world, and Śiva, who destroys it. It shows us the Creator conscious of the need to care for his work, but especially dependent on Viṣṇu, who from the Vaishnavite or Krishnaite viewpoint must remain the supreme god to whom all the other gods are submitted. Note that Brahmā is mentioned here under his name *ātma-bhū*, 'He who is born from himself (or by himself),' because the Creator cannot be the creation of anyone else, even if periodically he emerges from the lotus growing out of the navel of Viṣṇu at the beginning of each new cycle. According to the introductory chapter of the *Laws of Manu*, he is *hiraṇyagarbha*, the golden embryo, an egg resplendent like the sun which emerges from a seed deposited in the primordial waters, and who is the first personal manifestation of the supreme Being. Put more simply, Brahmā's concern here is to balance the *guṇa*. The world, symbolized here by a sinking boat, has become too tamasic and may founder before its appointed time. Hence the need for the sattvic intervention of Viṣṇu to alleviate the weight of this boat burdened by a population of unworthy, wicked and unrighteous men, as Swami Tapasyananda says (1980: 1, 36), so that it may arrive safely at the end of the *mahāyuga*, the traditional length of the four ages assigned to each humanity. Only then can Śiva really accomplish his work of dissolving the world (*pralaya*).

It would be tedious to repeat here the question of time, which we treated in a general fashion above (v. 11) by entering into the details of the eras of the world, as described in the *Purāṇa*. Readers wishing to know more may consult, for example, an original book by Gaston Georgel on the four ages of humanity (see bibliography). But we would like to point out the following: according to the *Purāṇa* we are currently at the end of the seventh of fourteen *manvantara* that make up a day of Brahmā.[60] To use a well-known image of popular science we can say that, according to this fantastic clock, it is noon minus one second, that is to say, the time it takes to blink before the seventh dissolution (*pralaya*) of our world on the day in question.[61] To make these notions fit in with an improbable scientific truth is of no special interest. But metaphysically the intention seems clear. The myth places man at the centre of time, that is, in the middle of the life of Brahmā, in the same way that it places him at the centre of space. This is connected to the concept of geocentrism and to the idea that the sacred territory of India, or any other country for that matter, is, according to tradition, considered the centre of the world. We do not live at the periphery, but at the exact time and place

60 This day is actually the first of the fifty-first year of the life of this god, which is limited to one hundred years.

61 According to oft-repeated Puranic calculations, the *kali-yuga* should last 432,000 solar years. Now, its origin, according to the *Sūrya-siddhānta*, a treatise on astronomy 1,600 years old, is usually dated February 18, 3102 BC, which brings us to 5114 (2012), a date that appears on many popular calendars in India. This would leave 426,886 years to go before the final dissolution, which seems exorbitant. Georgel, inspired by René Guénon (2003: ch. 1), offers an interesting downward revision of the calculation, while respecting the spirit of the tradition (1976: 56ff.). Note also that, according to most of the sources, it takes 71 cycles for four ages to form one *manvantara*.

where deliverance from *saṃsāra* is possible, and this is precisely what makes the human condition so precious. The myth is set in the present, and this present is like a point of eternity in time. In other words we must realize that this is potentially the beginning of the world in the sense that the origin is principial. As stated by Coomaraswamy: '"In the beginning" (*agre*), or rather "at the summit", means "in the first cause", just as in our still told myths, "once upon a time" does not mean "once" alone, but "once for all"' (1971: 6). The evocation of a fabled past has an ontological function. In addition, the fall in time envisaged by the doctrine of the four ages is necessarily accompanied by a fall into matter, which ends in its extreme thickening and solidification, preventing any further spiritual outcome for the world. This is followed by a phase of dissolution that brings about a catastrophe—in the etymological sense of 'a reversal'—which leads up to the emergence of a new Golden Age. Thus, the cycle lasts only insofar as there is still a possibility of salvation for man. The imminence of this major event puts humanity in an extremely urgent situation, which is acknowledged by all the currently extant religions.

For Guénon it is clear that humanity has already entered this phase of dissolution. In his chapter 'Towards Dissolution' in *The Reign of Quantity and the Signs of the Times*, he masterfully likens the transition of the materialist solidification characteristic of the modern era to what he calls a 'pulverisation', thus employing an alchemical term. Having recourse to this knowledge enables him to show what the process contains both negatively, relative to the end of the world, and positively, with respect to the genesis of a new cycle. He cites in this connection the *dies irae*, whose famous formula *solvet saeclum in favilla, teste David cum Sibylla*, '(that day) will reduce the world to ashes, according to the testimony of David and the Sibyl,' makes reference to both the Hebrew prophet and the ancient Sibyl. 'And this in itself is one of the ways,' says Guénon, 'in which the unanimous agreement of the different traditions is confirmed' (1972: 352).

The idea that the earth needs to be relieved of its burgeoning population is recurrent in the *Mahābhārata:* 'It is indeed to deliver the Earth plagued by overpopulation—the *Mahābhārata* repeatedly explains this in several ways—that Brahmā decides on a great bloodletting and orders the gods to incarnate to fulfil this' (Dumézil, 1986^5, 169, transl. DB). The same author also highlights this issue by naming the first part of his *Mythe et épopée*, which is devoted almost exclusively to Indian mythology, 'The Earth Relieved'. One also finds the same idea in the Greek tradition of the Trojan War: '... for the gods by means of Helen's loveliness embroiled Troy and Hellas, causing death thereby, that they might lighten mother Earth of the outrage done her by the increase of man's number' (Euripides, *Orestes*, 1639–42, translated by E. P. Coleridge). There is no doubt that in the Hindu imagination the current population explosion will in its turn call sooner or later for another cataclysm, which, in the Puranic view, may be just around the corner for present humanity. And it cannot be a *pralaya* comparable to that which separated the third from the fourth age.[62] We are

62 The *Mahābhārata* gives the clearly symbolic figure of 18 million dead in the war of Kurukṣetra, which if taken literally

on the eve of a great dissolution, a *mahāpralaya*. The traditional iconography of the event sometimes shows a terrible ogre swallowing entire cities in a single bite. After Hiroshima and Nagasaki this is no longer fiction.

18. *Still others (think thou wert born) so that the hearing, memory and reverence (of and for thy beneficent actions), may come to the aid of those who suffer in this world.*

Here is another verse which is particularly difficult to translate, especially with reference to the benefits of the coming of the avatar. For all the words have both a complex general and particular or even technical meaning. This is primarily the case with the idea of hearing (*śravaṇa*), a word derived from the root *ŚRU*, to hear, whose most well-known derivative, *śruti*, means audition.[63] This word is sometimes translated as revelation, because it refers to all the traditional writings (mainly the *Veda, The Visions*) considered as having inspired the *ṛṣi*, literally the seers, who 'heard' and transmitted them. Let us first address the question of this clash of the metaphors of hearing and vision. Hearing and sight being the two most precious human faculties, they are naturally,

---

appears an enormous number for such a remote time. The number 18 refers in particular to the 18 books of the epic, the 18 chapters of the *Bhagavad-gītā*, the 18 divisions of the armies engaged in the battle and the 18 days of the war, but also, according to some, to the 18 priests of the Vedic sacrifice, that is, the main pair (cf. v. 3) and their 16 followers.

63 This root corresponds etymologically to the Greek *kluo* and the old Latin word *cluo* or *clueo* found in *inclutus*, meaning 'famous' or 'of which one has heard'. The German word *laut* and the English loud, referring as they both do to sound, are equally related to this root.

in India as elsewhere, used as a symbol of a knowledge which, in reality, goes far beyond them. What the avatar enables us to hear, therefore, is situated on several different levels. What is heard first of all is what he said directly, but failing that, if we are not a contemporary, his words as they have been transmitted to us through stories of his life. This phenomenon is quite similar to what we said earlier about *darśana* (v. 8), where it is a question of those people who were privileged to have seen the avatar in his lifetime and those who could only contemplate him in his representations. What Kṛṣṇa said constitutes thus, for posterity, a spiritual teaching whose essence is contained in the *Bhagavad-gītā*, which occupies a central place in the *Mahābhārata* (6, 830–1532). The fact that this text is possibly a late addition, as suggested by some modern critics, is without relevance from the traditional point of view.

Then we hear the story of his adventures, which are obviously not just anecdotal, since they are also rich in various teachings. We have seen above (p. 17) that a ritual reading of the *Bhāgavata-purāṇa* exists. The *Bhagavad-gītā* is also recited daily by many Hindus. The basis of this practice is explained by Kṛṣṇa Himself: 'He who meditates on this sacred (*dharmya*) dialogue between you and me, worships me by performing the sacrifice of knowledge (*jñāna-yajña*). Such is my thinking. And the man who only hears it with faith and without malice, is also released. He reaches the blessed worlds of the righteous' (18, 70–71). The inherent blessing in the study or recitation of the sacred text extends, *mutatis mutandis*, to the entire *Mahābhārata*. Thus Vyāsa concludes his work by saying that whoever reads or hears this story, especially at every new moon, washes away his sins, purifies himself, becomes a better person and attains to Heaven. This belief is so alive in India that readers are willingly paid to provide the illiterate access to it or simply to make the text 'live' orally. Because, if the book containing the sacred text is necessarily a precious object, requiring respectful handling and a form of veneration, it is in the reciting and hearing of the revelation it vehicles that it becomes an effective means of transformation for man, or salvation, if you will.[64] Therefore, to read or to have someone read this book is called a *sādhanā*, a meritorious spiritual practice justified, in the final analysis, by the mention of the Name or Names of the avatar included in the text, which contain and mysteriously deliver the essence of his person, by virtue of the divine *māyā*: *kalikāle nāmarūpe kṛṣṇāvatāra*: 'In the *kali-yuga*, Kṛṣṇa incarnates (or, more literally, descends) in his Name' (cf. v. 8).

We find, lastly, in the idea of remembrance (*smaraṇa*)—mentioned in verse 8—a gradation similar to that applied to hearing: the devotee remembers the teaching embodied in the words and actions of the avatar, and he lives continually in his presence, which is rendered effective by the recitation of his Name. *Smaraṇa* mobilizes the intelligence, the soul and the will. The re-

---

64 It is the same, of course, for all the scriptures that 'existed' in the oral tradition before being put in writing. The word Qur'ān, for example, means recitation, and the book itself that contains this revelation is called in Arabic *muṣḥaf*, 'a collection of pages'. 'The Qur'ān does not speak, it is only a book made of paper, it is man who makes it speak,' 'Alī, quoted by E. Geoffroy (2009: 124).

membrance in question has little to do with the past in which the divinity manifested himself, but it is rather an ontological remembrance of our origin and our intimate and fundamental reality. The power of this remembrance is such that the *Bhāgavata-purāṇa* does not hesitate to say that it was because Kaṃsa, who, desperate to kill Kṛṣṇa since his birth to avoid his own demise, did not stop thinking about him whether sitting, lying, standing, eating, or moving, to the point that he saw the whole world penetrated by him, that he was saved at the moment of his death (10, 2, 24).

19. *Men who constantly listen to the story of thy acts, who sing them, who invoke thee, who remember thee, who rejoice in thee, these men contemplating thy lotus feet instantly gain cessation of the cycle of births and deaths.*

In this verse Kuntī again defines almost exhaustively the various approaches of the way of *bhakti*. The order of verbs is certainly not without significance. The first action of the devotee consists in listening to a teaching, that is, one that contains the account of Kṛṣṇa's life. The word that we translate as 'acts' contains the idea of desire, of intention. We are encouraged by that to understand what the avatar intended in his intervention in the affairs of men. While the *jñānin* takes as the starting point of realization an inner consciousness of an essentially metaphysical truth, the devotee follows *a priori* a concrete example of behaviour, of an incarnated truth, whose attraction he experiences as if by magic, a magic that is symbolized in particular by Kṛṣṇa's flute (cf. v. 8). His love and devotion are directed towards a personal God, an *iṣṭa-devatā*, as discussed earlier (p.26).

It is then required of him to sing the blessings of the Lord, to invoke Him and remember Him.[65] One can compare these actions to the attitudes mentioned in the divine commandment quoted by Jesus: 'Thou shalt love the Lord thy God with all thy heart, and with all thy soul and with all thy mind' (Matthew 22:37),[66] except that the first two elements seem to be reversed in the two traditions. When someone sings, he creates a vibration which radiates a presence throughout his soul. When he invokes, he affirms this Presence by an act of will that actualises it in his heart, and in remembering Him he fixes Him in his mind. All this culminates in the joy mentioned by Kuntī, in a converging upsurge expressed in the words of the Apostle: 'Rejoice evermore. Pray without ceasing' (1 Thess. 5:16–17). What most closely approximates Paul's injunction in the Queen's Hymn is the fact that, in both cases, it is stated that the act of the devotee, conceived as an act of joy, must be done constantly, without ceasing. Here we can see the esoteric interpretation which consists in taking for object of devotion, not the daily acts of the avatar, but his Name, which represents the quintessence of his person. It is not required of the *bhakta* that he 'recite without ceasing' Kṛṣṇa's actions, or 'remember all the time' the least details of his innumerable doings and exploits,

---

65 Actually this verse can be read on two levels. Kuntī speaks of men who hear, sing, invoke, remember and rejoice in the actions (or intentions) of Kṛṣṇa. But as we have seen above, the role of the avatar can be summarized in his person first of all and then in his Name. Our interpretation does not follow the text exactly word for word, but plays on the two meanings.

66 Mark adds: 'and with all your strength' (12:30).

even though there might be some merit in this, but that he live constantly in His Presence by invoking His Name.[67] One day someone asked a sage how it was possible to live simply, with all the material constraints involved, without straying from this constant activity of concentration on the divine Name. He answered that a mother busy with a thousand chores never for a minute forgets her baby sleeping in the adjoining room, and that at the slightest sound the needs of the baby become the centre of her concern again, as if he had never ceased to be present in her mind.

He who says perseverance, evokes the fight against time which devours the soul, and the distractions which disturb it. In the religious life of India, the necessary commitment to the way is supported and encouraged by the practice of many daily rituals which are contained in sometimes very simple actions, such as the offering of a flower or the burning of a stick of incense before the image of a deity. Some tourists are surprised or amused to see that in the great temples the Hindu priests dress the statues in rich garments which they sometimes change several times a day. Apart from the fact that after the rite of consecration the deity is supposed to inhabit its image which from then on is considered to be living, this practice aims to renew the motivation of the devotee by working on his imagination. This diversity responds

---

67 We mentioned earlier (v. 9) the role played by the Sufi *dhikr* as compared to *smaraṇa*. To be more precise, it must be said that this Qur'ānic notion covers both the idea of *smaraṇa* (memory) and that of *japa* (invocation). In other words, it is both an act of the intelligence and the will. This is why one can translate this Arabic term in two ways in both Sanskrit and English.

to the dispersing elements within the soul and therefore offers it multiple themes of meditation.

To return to the verse before us, we could also add that the Queen has thus defined, *a contrario*, the failings opposed to *bhakti-yoga*. Anyone who does not listen shows self-sufficiency or pride, he who does not sing shows coldness, who does not invoke, laziness, who cannot remember, forgetfulness, and who does not rejoice, bitterness. This list may suggest the deadly sins of the Christian tradition, whose limitation to seven in number seems, no matter what they say, somewhat arbitrary.[68] Why are forgetfulness of God, blasphemy or neglect, for instance, not deadly sins? According to Augustine, original sin is a sin of curiosity (*audax curiositas*), and in the case of Adam following Eve, it even seems to be a kind of conjugal weakness (*amicalis benevolentia*; see *De genesi ad litteram*, 11, 31, 41 and 11, 42, 60). In this selection, the importance of the number seven has certainly played a role which echoes the assertion of Proverbs (24:16), that the just man falls seven times a day. Perhaps this saying created a need to name these seven causes of the fall.

Similarly, a certain flexibility exists in the Indian tradition in relation to these obstacles to the spiritual path. The wise prince Prahlāda, persecuted by his father, and whose tribulations provoked the ire of Viṣṇu who incarnated as Narasiṃha, the man-lion, in order to save him, lists in the *Bhāgavata-purāṇa* (7, 5, 23–24) nine conditions for accomplishing the path of *bhakti*, the neglect

---

68 This did not escape Martin Lings who has written a very personal reflection on this list (2006: 86–97).

of which constitutes just as many 'cardinal sins'. As for Rūpa Gosvāmī, the disciple of the great Bengali saint Caitanya (cf. ch. 2) and the first Krishnaite theorist, he mentions six major hazards on the way, where excessive zeal (*prayāsa*), gossip (*prajalpa*), obstinate compliance to the rules (*niyamāgraha*) and seeking the company of profane men (*janasaṅga*) are set alongside greed and envy (*Upadeśāmṛta*, 2). This gives credence to the opinion that there may be a degree of uncertainty in this domain.

The perseverance required of the devotee, which develops over time, establishes man in the present moment, and hence the instantaneity (*acireṇa*) of the total cessation of the sequence of transient states (*bhava*) characterizing *saṃsāra* leads to the contemplation of the lotus feet of the avatar. That is, according to Hindu tradition, true deliverance (*mokṣa*) which releases the soul of the victim of the cosmic illusion from the indefinite cycle of rebirths.

20. *Now that thou hast accomplished what thou didst intend to do, O mighty Lord, wilt thou abandon us, we thy friends who live only by thee, we who have no other refuge but thy lotus feet, while the kings of the world plunge us into anxiety?*

In this verse, as in the next two, the Queen is concerned about the imminent departure of Kṛṣṇa, who is ready to return to his kingdom of Dvārakā, far from the Pāṇḍava. Even though he is still young, and the fact is that the epic does not make him die for another thirty-six years, the anguish of his final disappearance from the world as an avatar permeates Kuntī's petition. This is why she addresses her nephew in naming him with a new name, *prabhu*, a word frequently used in

Sanskrit literature and translated in many different ways in English or Western versions. It contains the ideas of power, wealth, excellence, and abundance, and we have rendered it as 'mighty Lord', which is neither better nor worse than many other possibilities. But if we look at the etymology, it can be argued that it means one who is born, who gushed forth, who manifested himself, who has become present. As such, this name is therefore appropriate in this context, and we have already pointed out the fact that the names of the gods or heroes are never chosen at random in the epic, but always illustrate a subtle aspect of the character highlighted in a given situation.

Since we are implicitly talking here of Kṛṣṇa's future demise, it is perhaps worth recalling briefly the circumstances of his strange end. Having lost her one hundred sons in the battle of Kurukṣetra, Gāndhārī, the Afghani[69] wife of the blind King Dhṛtarāṣṭra, curses Kṛṣṇa and predicts the end of all the Yādava, the descendants of Yadu, of whom Kṛṣṇa is the most illustrious representative (cf. ch. 1). Thus, long after the war, the avatar, knowing his time has come, gives a final teaching to his friend, the wise Uddhava.[70] And foreseeing that the ocean will swallow his capital, he advises his people to emigrate to the west, to Prabhāsa, by following the river Sarasvatī. Un-

69 That is to say, coming from the country of Gandhāra, in Afghanistan today. According to hermeneutical etymology, *gāṃ-dhārī* is the carrier or bearer of a cow, or the Carrier of the Earth, if one gives it its symbolic equivalence (cf. Biardeau 2002: II, 825).

70 This form of teaching dialogue, called *Uddhava-gītā*, occupies chapters 6–19 of the 11th book of the *Bhāgavata-purāṇa*.

fortunately, one evening, during a stop on the banks of the river, the Yādava begin to drink heavily, and in a drunken brawl kill each other. Only Kṛṣṇa and Balarāma survive by hiding in a forest. While the latter is sitting on a rock, a huge serpent, the famous Śeṣa whom he incarnates, comes out of his mouth and discards his lifeless body. Now alone, Kṛṣṇa assumes his form with the four arms and lies down on the ground. A hunter who is passing by, Jara (the Old One), mistakes his feet for the ears of a sleeping antelope and lets loose a fatal arrow. Before dying, the avatar still has time to promise deliverance to his unfortunate slayer and ask his charioteer, who has come in search of him, to take his body back to Dvārakā. All the gods, with Brahmā, Śiva and Indra at their head, gather around his funeral pyre. None of them can see where his spirit goes, in the same way that men cannot follow the trajectory of a flash of light. Then the ocean floods the city, leaving only the place of his funeral pyre to emerge (*Bhāgavata-purāṇa*, 11, 30–31) at the spot where the temple in present day Dwarka still stands commemorating this event and attracting countless pilgrims. Perhaps the most astonishing thing in this terrible tragedy is that Jara aims specifically at the lotus feet of the avatar.

The last point to make about this verse concerns the importance the Queen gives to her total dependence on Kṛṣṇa. The war has been won, at an exorbitant price, it is true, but her sons are now masters of the situation. All five are formidable fighters who no longer have any other opponent to fear besides Aśvatthāman, whom they have made the mistake of releasing but whom they have neutralized. The presence of Kṛṣṇa, even as a non-combatant, therefore seems less necessary than before. This again leads us to an esoteric interpretation of Kuntī's prayer. She does not address him as a powerful ally or as a military strategist, but as the Kṛṣṇa who revealed himself to Arjuna during the episode of the *Bhagavad-gītā*. She sees him as her only refuge (*parāyaṇa*). It is interesting to note in this regard that the term *parāyaṇa* is found in a famous dialogue related in the *Bṛhadāraṇyakopaniṣad* (3, 9, 1), where Śākalya asks the sage Yājñavalkya how many gods there are. The sage begins by telling him there are three thousand, three hundred and six. But at the insistence of his disciple who repeats the question several times, he brings the number down to thirty-three, then six, then three, then two, then one and a half, and finally one, who is none other than the *brahman*, who is called *tyad*, 'that', the absolute.[71] He then states that *tyad* is none other than the *parāyaṇa*, that is to say, the 'principle' of every *ātman*. The translator is naturally led to use the word refuge in the devotional climate of *bhakti* and the word principle in the sapiential context of the *Upaniṣad*, but it is the same Sanskrit word that is used in both instances, and this is where *bhakti-yoga* and *jñāna-yoga* converge.[72]

21. *What will become of us, we mere individuals, we Pāṇḍava and Yādava, when thou who art the Master of the senses, are no longer visible?*

---

71 Yājñavalkya systematically gives the names of the thirty-three gods, then six, and so on. He thus develops a theology whose base is still Vedic.

72 We have already encountered this term (v. 8) in an eloquent passage from the *Bhagavad-gītā*.

We have just seen, on the basis of an example borrowed from the use of terminology, how ultimately the paths of devotion or love and knowledge necessarily meet.[73] The question put by Kuntī in her distress provides a new and particularly interesting illustration of this reality. The word she uses to define her own individual condition and that of her relatives is *nāma-rūpa*, literally 'name and form'. Swami Tapasynanda translates this double term by the words 'reputation and prosperity': '... what will be the status of us, the Yadu and the Pāṇḍava, who have attained to reputation and prosperity...' This interpretation is not an error in the sense that it corresponds to the tone of the imagery and narrative of the epic, but the notion of *nāma-rūpa*, recurrent in the *Brāhmaṇa* and the *Upaniṣad*, has a metaphysical dimension that should also be taken into consideration. As Guénon states: 'The individual being is regarded in its totality as a compound of two elements called respectively "nāma" name and "rūpa" form, which in effect represent the "essence" and the "substance" of the individuality...' (2002: 152).[74] He then adds that this distinction is not

73 To the two paths mentioned here should be added, in accordance with the Hindu tradition as it appears in the *Bhagavad-gītā* as in many other texts, a third way, that of sacrificial action or works (*karma-yoga*). It is understood that any *sādhaka*, any person engaged in the spiritual life, follows the three paths simultaneously, but the focus is necessarily on the practice of one of these three ways. It also goes without saying that this triple perspective has its equivalents in all religious traditions.

74 He then compares these two elements to the Aristotelian form (*eidos, forma*) and matter (*hulē, materia*) with the nuance in terminology that form refers to *nāma* and matter to *rūpa*. We

without analogy to that which in the Western tradition is called the soul and body, it being understood that the concept of *rūpa* encompasses more than mere bodily form.

In other words, Kuntī asks Kṛṣṇa what happens to the soul and the body once separated from the spirit, thus making an implicit allusion to her own death as well as that of her family. She also calls her interlocutor the Master of the senses, using a synonym of the word that we encountered earlier (v. 6), which allows her to focus on the importance of the spirit as a single agent in relation to the individual being. The implicit answer to this is thus, according to Hindu tradition, twofold. If the person does not obtain deliverance at the time of death, the individual being continues to exist indefinitely in another mode. But if deliverance is attained at this ultimate moment, then in that case *brahman* will be known for what it is, in other words it will be realized, and then the *nāma-rūpa* will cease to exist, at least as a limitation. This is compared by some commentators of the *Brahma-sūtra* to water sprinkled on a boiling hot stone which evaporates so that it can no longer be seen. It then expands beyond all limits, having actually achieved its full potential (cf. Guénon 1945: 139–140). It is important to emphasize, however, the fact that it is only 'from the point of view of manifestation' that it appears to be an act of destruction or annihilation; for supreme realization cannot be a nothingness in itself, as nothingness is by definition unrealizable. In fact,

---

will see further on (v. 23) how Guénon also gives a macrocosmic meaning to the terms 'essence' and 'substance'.

the *nāma-rūpa* is reintegrated in this realization to its celestial or eternal prototype,[75] and the proof of this is that the *jivan-mukta*, the liberated living being, may elect to continue to 'live' in his body as long as it still retains its vital force.

Significantly then, the *bhakta's sādhanā*, his spiritual path, becomes a question. The avatar is there, he has become incarnate to deliver his teaching to men. And the question that Kuntī asks him, 'What will become of us (*ke vayam*) as *nāma-rūpa*?', is exactly the same question that Ramaṇa Maharṣi (cf. v. 3) directed his disciples to ask themselves insistently: *ko'ham*, 'Who am I?'[76] It is, in the *jñānika* context, what one calls *vicāra-yoga*, the path of questioning. The answer is of course that our true self is beyond the *nāma-rūpa*. It is the cosmic illusion that makes us identify with our body, our ego, our thoughts, our desires, losing sight of the fact that our only true Self is none other than the Master of the senses, the only real agent. There is no true consciousness outside of this. 'Losing sight' is exactly how it is expressed by Kuntī: *bhavato adarśanam yarhi*, literally: 'if there is no sight of your Lordship'.[77] We have seen above the

---

75 On this fundamental issue, we refer to the chapter 'Nirvana' by Frithjof Schuon (1993: 83–93).

76 *Ko'ham* is the first person singular: 'Who (am) I?' *Ke vayam* is the first person plural: 'Who (are) we?'

77 Amazing parallel with Guénon: '... the being who has transcended the human state by rising up the axis to the higher states is, so to speak, "lost to view" to everyone remaining in that state who has not yet reached its centre (and this includes everyone who is an initiate, but at a lower grade of initiation than the grade of "true man")' (1991: 126). As we have just seen

importance of *darśana* and its symbolic dimension of knowledge (v. 8). The Hindu *ke vayam* or *ko'ham* is the equivalent of the 'Know thyself' of Greek philosophy,[78] and Kuntī's question is a rhetorical one transmitting, in the language of the epic, a purely metaphysical truth. This evidence shows once more, if that is at all necessary, the relevance of hermeneutics aimed at considering all the characters of such sacred texts as being a part of ourselves, illustrating as they do the drama unfolding within us. It also shows, as in the previous verse, the goal common to the path of knowledge and the path of love.

22. *The earth, O Bearer of the mace, will no longer shine then, as it shines today trodden by thy feet that leave their footprints.*

Kṛṣṇa is designated here by the name Bearer of the mace (*gadādhara*), an allusion to one of the two weapons he wields as the incarnation of Viṣṇu, the other one being the discus. The symbolism of the mace is interpreted differently depending on the source. It is the knowledge that destroys all vain chimeras, but it is also Kāla, Time, the destroyer. It is with this weapon that Kṛṣṇa kills Kaṃsa, who, according to some, is also an incarnation of the *kali-yuga*, like Duryodhana who is also killed by a mace, namely Bhīma's (cf. v. 12). So only Time will definitely put an end to the Dark Age. This double slaying also leads to a double redemption, since not only is Kaṃsa delivered at the time of his death, but also

---

in the previous verse, Kṛṣṇa once cremated on his funeral pyre, is also lost to view by the other gods present.

78 The exact formula is found in the dialogue between Kṛṣṇa and Uddhava: 'Wherefore, O Uddhava, know thyself (or know thine *ātman*) through knowledge' (*Bhāgavata-purāṇa*, 11, 19, 1).

Yudhiṣṭhira meets the eldest Kaurava in Heaven, when he ascends there at the end of the epic. In this way the cosmic play justifies the behaviour of these two men who rebel against *dharma* and appear 'evil' in the eyes of men, in spite of the necessity of their role in the divine plan.[79]

Although we gave some keys to a microcosmic interpretation in the preceding verse, the allusion to the weapon of Viṣṇu and the earth marked by Kṛṣṇa's footprints naturally leads us here to a macrocosmic approach to the figure of the avatar. Kṛṣṇa, even if he is no longer living among men, remains in the world:

> 'I am the weft of all things, like the thread on which the pearls of a necklace are strung. O son of Kuntī, I am the taste in water, the light in the moon and the sun, the syllable *OM* in all the *Veda*, the sound in ether, and manliness in men. I am the sweet fragrance of the earth, the heat of the fire, the life in all creatures, the asceticism of ascetics' (*Bhagavad-gītā*, 7, 7–9).

To perceive Kṛṣṇa in this way, to see God everywhere, as the mystics say, is considered by some to be an even greater grace than actually seeing him physically as an avatar: '... blessed are they that have not seen, and yet have believed.' Thus, the gopis of Vṛndāvana are never more in love with their divine lover that when he leaves for Mathurā. These lovers separated from their beloved only think of him, and as their love grows, magnified by the pain of illusory separation, their *nāma-rūpa*, or

---

79 In the same way, Judas is as it were commissioned by Christ during the Last Supper, when he gives him a sop and says, 'That thou doest, do quickly' (John 13: 27).

distinct identity, is melted in Kṛṣṇa, like the sages in ecstasy (*samādhi*) or the rivers in the ocean (*Bhāgavata-purāṇa*, 11, 12, 12).

This macrocosmic or universal dimension of the avatar is at the centre of the speculations of a late *Upaniṣad*, the *Kṛṣṇopaniṣad*, which provides countless parallels that can be taken as keys to reading the epic. Thus, among other things, Devakī and Vasudeva, the natural parents of Kṛṣṇa, are equated respectively with the syllable *OM* and the whole text of the *Veda*, whose meaning is, for its part, personified by Balarāma. The sacred verses are identified with the sacred cows and the gopis who guard them; or else with the 16,108 women who become the lovers of the god. Brahmā, the creator, is embodied in Kṛṣṇa's mace, Rudra (Śiva) in his flute, and Indra in his conch. Alternatively, the latter emblem is also understood as an incarnation of Lakṣmī, the goddess of fortune and wife of Viṣṇu. The butter that Kṛṣṇa steals in his childhood, and which he gobbles, refers to the ocean of milk which Viṣṇu lies on between two creations, and which contains the causal world at the origin of all manifestation. The conch emits the primordial sound at the origin of the world, and the disc seals the fullness of the cycle at the end of each time period, and so on...[80] This profusion of correspondences shows how impossible it is to provide a systematic interpretation of Kṛṣṇa's actions. It also shows that this immense wealth of material is always open to new developments, which all inspired sages can

80 On this see Daniélou, 1992: 271–3.

use *ad libitum* until the end of time, as long as the spirit of the tradition is respected.

The end of the verse under consideration alludes to a somewhat similar symbolic hunting game, since here it is a question of footprints on the earth left by the feet of the avatar. The traditional iconography represents the soles of his feet adorned with different marks, such as the drawing of a flag, a discus, the hook of a mahout, a lotus, a thunderbolt, an umbrella, a crescent moon, a tree, a swan, a conch, a throne, a lute, and various people, etc.[81] The metaphor of the hunt is also therefore constantly present as we follow the footsteps of the avatar. The path is a hunting track (*mārga*), the expressions *bhakti-mārga* and *bhakti-yoga* being perfectly synonymous. Again, as Guénon says: '... From the human state, "transcendent man" can only be seen by his "trace", and this "trace" is identical to the figure of "true man". From this perspective, the one is indistinguishable from the other' (1991: 126). It may be that Guénon is making an allusion above all to a figurative trace, hence the use of quotation marks. In the Western tradition one speaks also, in this regard, of the *vestigium pedis*, a term which applies to all footprints left by a prophet or a saint, which are the object of veneration. Islam is also familiar with this symbol; the most famous example perhaps being

81 'The feet of Vishnu symbolize the unity of the entire universe. All the elements of the universe are represented by various auspicious signs indicating many aspects of the Ultimate One. As fundamentally all things are one, since they are only fragments of the Supreme Unity, they are to be regarded as symbols or emblems of a higher reality' (Mookerjee 1971: 54, and 55 for the illustration).

the prints left by the mysterious mare Al-Burāq when, according to some traditions, she leapt from the rock of the Al-Aqṣā Mosque in Jerusalem carrying the Prophet through the Heavens on his Night Journey to God. Also worth mentioning is the equally famous footprint of Adam on the highest mountain of Sri Lanka (Adam's Peak), which is also claimed by the Buddhists, who consider it a print of the Buddha's foot.

23. *All these happy people, this luxuriant vegetation, the forests, mountains, rivers, oceans, thrive only thanks to thy glance.*

In a poetic manner the Queen simply summarizes here the relationship that unites the two poles of manifestation, *puruṣa* and *prakṛti*, to which the whole of chapter 13 of the *Bhagavad-gītā* is devoted. The translation of these two words is quite problematic and Guénon, examining the question in detail (1945: 48), definitively rejects in this context the concepts of spirit and matter, tinged as they are with Cartesianism and therefore rendered unsuitable for describing Hindu thought. Using instead Aristotelian terminology (see n. 74 above), he proposes the terms essence and substance, from *eidos* and *hulē*, as being applicable to the entirety of manifestation.[82] As we saw in verse 11, in connection with the idea

82 'It is the first of all dualities, that from which all others derive directly or indirectly, and it is with this distinction that multiplicity strictly speaking begins: but one must not see in it the expression of an absolute irreducibility which is in no wise to be found there: it is Universal Being which, relatively to the manifestation, of which it is the Principle, polarises Itself into "Essence" and "Substance", without its intrinsic unity being however affected in any way thereby' (*ibid.*, p. 49). This is the point of view of *Vedānta*, which is essentially non-dualistic,

of the co-eternity of manifestation in relation to the principle, '*puruṣa* and *prakṛti* are both without beginning' and '*puruṣa*, established in *prakṛti*, enjoys the *guṇa* born of *prakṛti*' (*Bhagavad-gītā*, 13, 19 and 21). As a spectator (*upadraṣṭṛ*), *puruṣa* is passive, and *prakṛti*, engendering all manner of creation, is active. This is what Kuntī means in describing the beauties of nature unfolding under the benevolent gaze of Kṛṣṇa. But the opposite, namely that *puruṣa* is active and *prakṛti* is passive, is also true, since it is by the grace of Kṛṣṇa's gaze that nature thrives. The fact that man, at the present time, is systematically defiling nature is surely a sign for the Hindu, heralding the end of the *kali-yuga*, and a foretaste of the final dissolution, as if man in forgetting the role of Kṛṣṇa as *puruṣa* has veiled his beneficent glance.

Everything that is said in this verse is true not only in terms of the macrocosm, which the Queen explicitly refers to, but also in terms of the microcosm. Thus, 'This supreme *puruṣa* is called, in the body, the spectator and approver,[83] one that supports, the enjoyer, the great Lord, the supreme Self' (*Bhagavad-gītā*, 13, 22). It is perhaps worth recalling that the dialogue between Kṛṣṇa and Arjuna in the *Bhagavad-gītā* takes place on the eve of the battle between the Pāṇḍava and the Kaurava and, what is more, in a specific place between the two rivers of the Ganges and the Yamunā, midway between the capital of the Pāṇḍava, at Indraprastha, and the Kaurava,

---

while if the *Sāṃkhya* may seem dualistic, it is because it does not consider what goes beyond the duality of *puruṣa* and *prakṛti*, without for all that denying it.

83 Like the aesthete approving the execution of a musical work, glosses in substance Swami Chidbhavananda (1969: 702).

at Hāstinapura. This plain is called Kurukṣetra, the field of Kuru. In addition, the *kṣatriya*, the warrior, is etymologically 'the man of the field' (of battle), the *kṣetra*.

Now, Kṛṣṇa, in the chapter of the *Bhagavad-gītā* before us, identifies *prakṛti* and *puruṣa*, respectively, as the field and as himself insofar as he is the knower of the field: 'Know, O descendant of Bharata, I am the knower of the field (*kṣetrajña*) in all fields. The knowledge of the field and the knower of the field I consider to be (true) knowledge' (13, 2).[84] This field, he then says, is the body (*śarīra*). And he adds: 'This *kṣetra* is made up, briefly, of the (five) major subtle elements, the ego, the intellect, the undifferentiated, the ten senses, the inner sense and the five objects of the senses.[85] It is desire, hatred, pleasure, happiness, unhappiness, the aggregate of the body, thought, and will' (13, 5–6). Such is thus the real battlefield of the devotee of Kṛṣṇa, as it is for every spiritual man.

Returning from a military expedition, the Prophet said: 'We have returned from the lesser holy war to the greater holy war,' playing on the ambiguity of the word *jihād*, which refers to both martial combat and the far more important inner struggle within man. Thus

---

[84] Chapter 13 of the *Bhagavad-gītā* is variously entitled 'The *yoga* of discrimination between *prakṛti* and *puruṣa*' or '*Yoga* of the distinction between the field and the knower of the field.'

[85] The elements listed here will become the twenty-four principles of *Sāṃkhya*, plus *puruṣa*, though independent of them, as the twenty-fifth. The undifferentiated or undeveloped one is *prakṛti* which is not produced, but produces the other twenty-three principles. For more on this, we refer the reader to Guénon (1945) and to the *Sāṃkhya-kārikā*.

the term *jihād* covers the two meanings of the Latin *virtus* exactly. Both of these words mean firstly, physical courage, as shown in war, and secondly, virtue (precisely derived from *virtus*), that is to say, the fortitude necessary in the fight against the ego. The Prophet teaches us in this way that war in the military sense is to be understood as a symbol of the struggle against the negative tendencies of the soul. In doing this he is in perfect harmony with the teachings of the *Bhagavad-gītā* on the microcosmic dimension of the epic.

24. *O Lord of the universe, O Soul of the universe, O Form of the universe, cut this strong bond of affection which binds me to my family, the Pāṇḍava and Vṛṣṇi.*

Of the three names used here to describe Kṛṣṇa, we have already encountered the second (v. 13), and the meaning of the first (*viśveśa*) is already implicitly clear (*īśa* is a variant of *īśvara*, cf. v. 1). It remains to say a word about the third. Kṛṣṇa is called *viśva-mūrti*, the Form of the universe, the term *mūrti* designating all divine manifestation, as in the famous name *tri-mūrti*, applied to the triple manifestation of the gods Brahmā, Viṣṇu and Śiva.[86] It is precisely as *viśva-mūrti* or *viśva-rūpa* in his cosmic form that Kṛṣṇa appears on Arjuna's chariot. He then has countless bodies and innumerable faces. He fills all the space between heaven and earth, brandishing his many arms, spitting flames, swallowing and spitting out various creatures, etc. His companion is struck by a mixture of stupefaction and fear. Written in

---

86 It would be problematic to speak here of a trinity, due to the use of this term in Christianity, where it refers to a different theology.

a different metre to the rest of the dialogue, chapter 11 of the *Bhagavad-gītā*, which recounts this vision, is probably the most poetic in the whole work. Moreover, let us remember, for a proper understanding of this verse, that Kuntī, the mother of the Pāṇḍava, belongs also to the family of the Vṛṣṇi, another name for the Yādava clan.

It has already been mentioned that attachment to family can become an obstacle to the spiritual life (v. 10), and specifically, it is a sentiment like this that almost prevents Arjuna from doing his duty on the battlefield. We have also alluded in this context to the example of Nicolas de Flue, a Swiss saint of the 15th century who, after an exemplary family and civil life—he was even a soldier and fought in several battles—retired at the age of fifty to a hermitage close to home, where he remained for twenty years without eating or drinking, receiving many visitors, including major political and religious figures. His life was that of a typical *saṃnyāsin*, a renunciant, like the many in India, and his story has been enjoyed enormously by the Hindus to whom we could recount it.[87] Now, what is a *saṃnyāsin*? Brahmanical ideology considers that man can legitimately pursue four goals in life (see Introduction), namely material well-

87 For more details on this remarkable saint, little known outside his homeland, we refer the reader to the book by Cardinal Journet (see bibliography). A feature of his life that interests Hindus, in addition to his total fasting, is the fact that he did not leave his position as head of the family without ensuring their livelihood, entrusting the management of the farm to his eldest son. A married Hindu cannot become a *saṃnyāsin* without the permission of his wife and vice versa, this permission having the value of a blessing.

being, including health (*artha*); emotional well-being in marriage, as in all relations of kinship or friendship (*kāma*); honesty or morality, especially in professional life (*dharma*); and finally, ultimate deliverance from the illusion of the world (*mokṣa*). Now an apparent difficulty arises from the fact that the first three of these goals are concerned with the life here-below, seeming to contradict the fourth, which is aimed *de facto* at the afterlife. This paradox is, however, inherent in human nature. It is not because we know that we must die one day that we give up the enjoyment of earthly goods. What religion more demands of us, and in this the Indian tradition is no different from any other, is to realize that this life is only a dream, an illusion, and that we must be prepared to wake up from it one day.[88] Now, this awareness of the impermanence of the here and now must be cultivated even in ordinary life. It is only to the extent that we forget who we are that the attachments to family, like all others, have to be cut. That said, we know that in India a man or a woman can always withdraw from society at any age to live a hermit's life, often, but not necessarily, wandering about, and dedicated solely to the fourth order of existence that is deliverance. The person who makes this choice is, naturally, subject to some rules,[89]

---

88 The Prophet summarizes the proper attitude of man: 'Work for this world as if you were to live forever, and work for the Hereafter as if you were to die tomorrow.'

89 The wandering hermit usually travels from one pilgrimage site to another. He has, in principle, the right to beg his food only once from the same house and cannot stay longer than three days in one place. Obviously there are countless variations for people following this path.

and inaugurates this new state through a rite similar to a funeral, because he or she leaves society as a deceased person. He is then what in Latin is called a *defunctus*: one who ceases his social function.

But the practice of renunciation is not an obligation for the devout secular person except in the inward sense, and the immediate and uncompromising rejection of the first three goals of life depends on a particular vocation. Kṛṣṇa did not ask Arjuna to leave his wives and give up the fight. In fact quite the opposite: he urged him to fulfil his duty as a *kṣatriya*, but without regard to the fruits of action. This is called *niṣkāma-karman*, the accomplishment of acts without selfish desire for their fruits. 'Be always focused on your actions, never on their fruits. Do not have as aim the fruit of your actions, and do not let yourself be drawn to inaction' (*Bhagavad-gītā*, 2, 47). The *Bhagavad-gītā* contains a great many verses relating to this conception of renunciation, and chapter 5 is devoted entirely to this subject. In general, the ability to act without attachment to the fruit of the act is said to be, in India, the main feature distinguishing man from beast. The popular idea that a man can be reborn as an animal as long as he has not been sufficiently disinterested in the fruits of his actions has no other origin.

It is perhaps worth adding that there is also an implicit justification here of a sexuality independent of reproduction, raising man *de facto* above the animal. In the same way as the *kṣatriya* is expected to fight without caring for the fruits of his actions, because that is his function, so spouses are invited to unite without worrying about begetting offspring, like Rādhā and

Kṛṣṇa, whose example, even if it transcends common experience, cannot deny it purely and simply.[90] We also know the importance Tantra gives to this aspect of human existence. *A contrario* the *saṃnyāsin* does not so much give up having children as such, which is possible without abandoning all sexual activity, as seek to sublimate an energy whose power is considerable, to say the least.

That the renunciation required by *bhakti* should not automatically lead to the abandonment of work and family life is not only illustrated in the *Mahābhārata* by the example of Arjuna and other *kṣatriya* pushed into battle by Kṛṣṇa. The most astonishing example of this possibility perhaps is that of Yudhiṣṭhira. The eldest of the Pāṇḍava, and the son of the god Dharma, shows more than once in the epic his desire to leave his kingdom behind and embrace a hermit's life, but he is always deterred from doing this by his relatives or by circumstances. He lives out the strange drama of a king who seems to have little taste for power. But his renunciation consists precisely in this personal sacrifice for the benefit of his function, and it is perhaps from this that he takes his name Yudhiṣṭhira, which means in effect 'He who stands firm in the fight.' One could also say that by his renunciation of renunciation he enhances the nobility of the path of works, or that he was a monarch aware of the primacy of the greater holy war over the lesser holy war.

We mentioned earlier (v. 12) another example of re-

---

90 This, of course, did not stop Kṛṣṇa from also having children; Rukmiṇī, his 'first' wife, bore him ten sons.

nunciation, that of the gopis who leave their husbands to give themselves fully to Kṛṣṇa. As Coomaraswamy has said, we are here, in symbolic mode, in the presence of a real *saṃnyāsa* where sexual union represents the mystical union of the soul with God, insofar as it involves complete forgetfulness of self and social conventions. In later Hinduism, the total gift of self this represents has created an interesting iconographic rule: Rādhā, who is the perfect lover of Kṛṣṇa, is the only female character in the entire pantheon who is allowed to be represented naked, 'as God created her' (cf. v. 9), that is without the least jewel, which is also consistent with the interpretation of nudity given by Schuon concerning the theft of the saris (cf. v. 14).[91]

In fact, Hinduism places the ideal of renunciation so high that we find amazing illustrations of it everywhere in Indian society. Most untouchables believe that they are descended from a Brahmin who voluntarily surrendered his purity through devotion to the deity. One of them in Kerala told us, for example, that once the Goddess, who was having her period, asked a group of Brahmins if a member of their caste would wash her clothes soiled by menstrual blood. They all refused except one who, showing a greater devotion, accepted this task which was literally degrading as to his status, thus committing his descendants to a marginal existence. Myths of this type, with many variants, abound in almost all the *jāti* of the untouchables. They confer on these disadvantaged communities not only a legitimate social

---

[91] In Western art, this full nudity is, in contrast, very common, whether one thinks, in a religious context, of Eve or Mary of Egypt or, in a profane context, of all fine art.

status but also a pride in fulfilling a necessary social function.

25. *O Sovereign of Madhu, may my thoughts never have any other object than thee. May they find (in thee) their joy, like the Ganges flowing into the ocean.*

Kṛṣṇa is the Sovereign of Madhu, or rather the Mādhava, the descendants of Madhu, and inhabitants of Mathurā. But this name (Madhupati) is sometimes understood as a variant of Madhusūdana, the killer of Madhu, the name of a demon destroyed by the avatar. Whatever the interpretation, the word *madhu* means first, in its immediate sense, honey, and metaphorically, because a heady drink is made from honey,[92] the season of spring. Kṛṣṇa is therefore also the ruler of honey and of spring. He inebriates; he intoxicates his devotees by his beauty, his smile, his perfect ease and most importantly, as we have seen, by the sweetness of the tunes of his flute. This is certainly the case in his most common representations, as the adolescent cowherd, the bucolic god living in a rustic setting, reminiscent of the happiness of the first age, the *kṛta-yuga*, the perfect age. At this blessed time, intoxicating drinks such as *soma* were not prohibited, because man was not likely to forget God.[93] The representation of Kṛṣṇa is an essential part

[92] *Madhu* is related to the Greek *methu*, an intoxicating drink, a term that we find in the adjective methyl, for example.

[93] The Qur'ān forbids wine not because it is bad in itself, but because its disadvantages outweigh its benefits (2: 219). Muslims know that this drink is reserved for them in Paradise (47: 15) and Sufis sing of its virtues. Some followers of tantrism also drink alcohol.

of the life of the devotee, since, by becoming incarnate, the avatar offers men an image of God. *Bhakti*, and then tantrism which continued it, cannot be achieved without the support of such images, as *darśana* is inherent in these paths (see v. 8). Hinduism, whether bhaktic or tantric, is obviously not the only religion to give such importance to the worship of images. Among the world's great religions, others advocate this form of worship, starting with Catholic and Orthodox Christianity—Lutheranism and Protestantism, in contrast, reject this attitude—which is why the Christian religion has always been regarded by Hindus as a devotional way, a *bhakti*. This is obviously a simplification, but the veneration of the saints and the Virgin approaches this. Buddhism, with its representations of the Awakened One, the Buddha, as of numerous other saints and divine persons, especially in Tibetan *vajrayāna*,[94] and the idea of taking refuge in the Buddha, has a dimension that can also be included in this category. It would take us too far, however, from the subject to clarify here how Buddhist spirituality differs from Hinduism.[95] In contrast, Islam, with its

---

94 We know that at first there was no iconography of the Buddha, but nevertheless he was represented quite early on, probably under the influence of Hinduism. In Tibet, in contrast, where Buddhism arrived much later, there emerged from the beginning a plethora of images.

95 It is clear, as shown above all by Madeleine Biardeau, that the *Mahābhārata* was part of a movement which came in reaction to Buddhism, as has been mentioned in the Introduction. But we must not forget that it was primarily due to the Vedantic, and therefore typically jñānic, preaching of Śaṅkara, that Buddhism was expelled from India in the 8th century AD.

a priori aniconic viewpoint, is unquestionably rather a *jñāna-yoga*, a path of knowledge. As for Judaism, the first Abrahamic religion, it seems, with its ritualism, to represent a kind of karmic path like the Vedic religion.

There is not much to say about this verse that has not already been the subject of a commentary in the preceding pages. Kuntī summarizes here what she has been able to develop previously, and we are approaching the conclusion of her hymn of thanksgiving. Many quotations from the *Bhagavad-gītā* remind us, in one way or another, that the avatar embodies the one thing necessary which gives a purpose to life, the return of the contingent to the essential; in a word, to teach us who we are. 'May my thoughts (or my devotion, the word has both meanings) never have any other object than thee,' says Kuntī. Speaking thus, the Queen therefore only reminds us of the purpose of the human condition. As God says in the Qur'ān: 'I have only created Jinn and men that they may worship me' (51: 56).

Even though commenting on the *Bhāgavata-purāṇa* has made us focus on *bhakti-yoga*, we have not failed to note on several occasions that this path is not opposed to *jñāna-yoga*, which it necessarily includes in one way or another. Kuntī's prayer expresses in a devotional way what Śaṅkara states in a well-known sapiential formula: '*Brahman* is real, the world is false; the individual soul is not other than *brahman*' (*Brahmajñānāvalīmālā*, 20). Now, all this is already contained in the *Bhagavad-gītā*. Defining *brahman*, Kṛṣṇa says: 'I will tell you what is the object of knowledge. Anyone who knows this attains immortality. It is *brahman*, the Supreme, without beginning, who is said to be neither being nor nonbeing' (13, 12). And later, after explaining this truth, he concludes: 'My devotee who knows this attains to my being (*bhāva*)' (13, 18). The reader may ask what is the etymological meaning of *brahman*. This word, neuter in gender, is derived from the root *BṚH*, which means to grow. *Brahman* is that which grows indefinitely, without limit, and thus the term comes to designate the ultimate Reality, both infinite and absolute. The *brāhmaṇa*, the Brahmin, is one who knows this truth and therefore has the ability to formulate it, which explains why his name is derived from this root. *Brahman* becomes, in his mouth, the sacred word itself. As for Brahmā (a masculine word), he is the creator god who, by his action, actually 'grows' the world.

The metaphysics of Śaṅkara's formula, given above, is reminiscent in its first hemistich of the *shahāda*, the testimony of faith of Islam, namely that 'there is no god if not God.' Everything that we can think of outside of ultimate Reality is ephemeral or illusory. And the subsequent affirmation, namely that the individual soul is not other than *brahman*, suggests the second Islamic testimony, namely, that 'Muhammad is the Messenger of God.' As Universal Man, the Prophet reveals the fundamental unity between *brahman* and *jīvātman*: *Ahaṃ brahmāsmi*, 'I am *brahman*' (*Bṛhadāraṇyakopaniṣad*, 1, 4, 10), and *Tattvamasi*, 'That thou art' (*Chāndogyopaniṣad*, 6, 8, 7). The two components of Śaṅkara's statement, like the two testimonies, define respectively the doctrine and way, and thus address on the one hand the intelligence, and on the other, the will.

Lastly, in speaking of enjoyment (*rati*), Kuntī expresses herself in a language replete with sexual connotations, for the expression that we have rendered as 'finding joy' might well be translated as 'marrying pleasure', since this is another meaning derived from the root *ud-VAH*. There is here, like an underlying tone, an allusion to sexual union as a symbol of the supreme identity. The mention of the Ganges also evokes, but this time explicitly, a traditional symbol: beings, as individuals, are likened to drops of water falling from the clouds which the great sacred river of the tradition brings back, without obstacle, to the ocean from whence they came, and where 'they merge without being mingled,' in the words of Meister Eckhart. For such is the cycle of life and the eternal return.

26. *O blessed Lord Kṛṣṇa, O friend of Kṛṣṇa, O Bull of the Vṛṣṇi, O thou who without losing thy strength, destroyeth the dynasties of kings who harm the earth, O Govinda, O thou who dost put an end to the suffering of cows, initiates and gods, O Descent (of God on earth), O Lord of the way, O Master of the universe, O God, homage to thee.*

Such is the conclusion to Kuntī's hymn of thanksgiving, made up of a list of Kṛṣṇa's names, some of which we are already familiar with. The second mention of the name Kṛṣṇa actually refers here to Arjuna, because the latter had dark skin as a child, before he became known as the Brilliant, the Silver One.[96] In more than one respect, Arjuna is Kṛṣṇa's *alter ego*. When he meets the Pāṇḍava, Kṛṣṇa prostrates himself before Yudhiṣṭhira and Bhīma, his seniors, embraces Arjuna, his contempor-

---

96 The root *ARJ* means to shine, and is found in the Latin word *argentum*, silver. The word 'argument' ('clarifying an idea') derives from the same root.

ary, and receives the homage of Nakula and Sahadeva, his juniors, who in turn prostrate themselves before him. Two other characters of the epic also bear this name, and this is not without significance. There is first of all Vyāsa, the Diffuser, the designated author of the *Mahābhārata*, whose first name is Kṛṣṇa Dvaipāyana, 'He who is born on an island,' a reference to the circumstances of his birth. Draupadī also bears this name in the feminine, with the elongation of the final *ā* (Kṛṣṇā), which among other things recalls the special relationship that unites her with the avatar in the famous dice game scene (ch. 1).

The presence of four Kṛṣṇa, of four black deities in the epic, also leads to interesting interpretations by commentators, the most interesting being perhaps the one that sees in this quartet a personification of the three gods of the *trimūrti*, namely Brahmā, Viṣṇu and Śiva, and Devī; that is, the four main figures of the Hindu pantheon. Vyāsa, as the author of the epic and the substitute progenitor of Pāṇḍu and Dhṛtarāṣṭra, will then represent Brahmā, the creator god, while Kṛṣṇa is Viṣṇu, Arjuna is Śiva, and Draupadī is Devī (cf. Hiltebeitel 1991). If the first two of these equivalences appear obvious, it is more surprising to see Arjuna, the son of Indra, associated with Śiva. But he performs a specifically Śaivite function to the extent that he is the most formidable warrior on the battlefield. In addition, during his period of exile before the battle, he goes to the Himalayas especially to meet Śiva, from whom he gains his most terrible weapon, the *pāśupata*, a magic bow. When he fights with it he therefore carries the destructive power of the god. The case of Draupadī is a little curious.

In the Vaisnavite context, the Devī appears in the form of Lakṣmī, and the *Purāṇa* do much to portray Draupadī as a reincarnation of Sītā, who has precisely this function in the story of Rāma.[97] This means that, in principle, she should be the wife of Kṛṣṇa, and not Arjuna and his four brothers. We can therefore assume that in the *Mahābhārata*, on the eve of the Dark Age, Kṛṣṇa decides in some way to lend them his *śakti*, which agrees with the fact that he also refrains from fighting in the war. There may be a link here between the fact that Viṣṇu, incarnated as Rāma, at the end of the second age has to divorce his wife Sītā under pressure from some of his subjects, who question her purity after her abduction, and the even greater distancing of Kṛṣṇa vis-à-vis the Devī at the end of the third age. But we are here in the realm of pure speculation.[98]

Kṛṣṇa is, furthermore, Bull of the Vṛṣṇis, that is to say, their king, according to a current Sanskrit metaphor. We have already encountered several kings he destroyed in order to fulfil his mission of preserving *dharma*, because they defiled the earth with their outrageous behaviour. The initiated are the *dvija*, the twice-born, namely the members of the three castes, that is to say the Brahmins, the *kṣatriya* and the *vaiśya*, and the gods are the *sura* (cf. v. 16). With the exclusion of all the other creatures, the cows, the *dvija* and the *sura* represent respectively the animal, human and divine kingdoms, and are the

---

97 It will be recalled, on the one hand, that Sītā had to undergo the ordeal of fire and, on the other, that Draupadī was born of the sacrificial fire precisely.

98 Besides the fact that in the *Mahābhārata* Kṛṣṇa is still the husband of Lakṣmī in her incarnation as Rukmiṇī.

pillars that maintain the cosmic order, each in its own realm. For the first time here, Kṛṣṇa is explicitly named as being of divine descent (*avatāra*). Finally, he is God, *bhagavat*, the Fortunate, the Prosperous, the Adorable, as the *Bhagavad-gītā* describes him in its title.[99]

[99] In the *Bhāgavata-purāṇa* we find, with the elongation of the first *ā*, the corresponding adjective: *The Lordly Purāṇa*. Note that God is called *Bok* in Slavic languages, a term derived from the same root.

Conclusion

The publisher of a well-known orientalist celebrated the merits of his protégé by saying that he derived his knowledge of India from having lived there, and not from basing it on the niceties of philologists who dissect words. If it is obvious that direct contact with the atmosphere and the way of life of India appears necessary in order to speak about it with authority, we do not see why he had to denigrate a careful study of the language and the substance of the texts. The Sanskrit language is considered sacred by Hindus, and they themselves engage in a sophisticated speculation on its letters and lexicon, including a hermeneutic technique of interpretation called *nirukta*, by which means they reveal the incomparable riches of this metaphorical and symbolic language. Although we have enlarged on their point of view in using arguments from other sources, we have not acted differently from them. It must be said that the West, attracted as it is by the Indian tradition, is faced with a significant challenge, given the enormous amount of material available. Who has read the entire *Mahābhārata*, even in an abridged version? Who has read an entire translation of the *Bhāgavata-purāṇa*, or the entire corpus of the *Upaniṣad*? One is quickly tempted, since time is passing more rapidly than ever, to skim these works and see them as verbose *amplificatio*, to use a classical rhetoric term. But we believe, on the contrary, that by having dwelt on a brief passage we have shown that within the abundant riches of the epic the essential is never forgotten, and that the coherence of the doctrine is present in every detail of the story. Better without doubt to read a little section carefully, than to consume thoughtlessly hundreds of pages.

Kuntī's speech of thanksgiving is thus, despite its brevity, a sort of condensed version of the *Bhagavad-gītā* which summarizes its key lessons with perfect orthodoxy. While our commentary on the epic has been necessarily situated in the domain of *bhakti*, we have seen that this general coloration does not shut the door to other ways or approaches. The Hindu tradition, which is always more inclusive than exclusive, offers exceptional lessons for seekers of all descriptions. When the Queen had finished speaking, Kṛṣṇa simply accepted her speech with his ineffable smile, and then left the Pāṇḍava for Dvārakā.

Appendix: Summary of the *Mahābhārata*

Only the central outline of the epic is retold here in order to facilitate an overall understanding of the commentary. More precise episodes are detailed in the course of the work, and the interested reader is referred to the books listed under *Mahābhārata* in the bibliography.

ॐ

Śāntanu, the king of the lunar Bhārata dynasty, reigns over a large territory situated in the north of India. His capital is Hāstinapura, the Town of the Elephant, on the banks of the Ganges. Desirous of obtaining an heir, he first of all has an affair with the goddess Gaṅgā, who gives him a strong and virtuous son called Bhīṣma. But the goddess leaves him and he falls madly in love with Satyvatī, the daughter of the King of the Fish, who agrees to give his daughter to Śāntanu on the express condition that it will be one of their sons, in other words a son of his own line, who will inherit the kingdom. Out of reverence for his father, the magnanimous Bhīṣma, legitimate heir to the throne, renounces power and even marriage in order to avoid any conflict which could be caused by the birth of direct offspring from the older line of the dynasty he represents.

Satyavatī thus marries Śāntanu and gives him two sons who die before coming to the throne, and what is more, before they can even beget descendants. In despair at this, she confesses that she has already had, thanks to a clandestine affair with a Brahmin, a son called Kṛṣṇa Dvaipāyana. This dirty and unkempt hermit will, under the name of Vyāsa, become the author of the *Mahābhārata*. She gets her husband to agree that Vyāsa sleep with the two sisters who had been married to her younger son, now deceased, in an attempt to save the line of the King of the Fish.

With the first of the wives of his half-brother, Vyāsa begets Dhṛtarāṣṭra, who is unfortunately born blind because his mother, Ambikā, disgusted by the repulsive looks of the hermit, had shut her eyes during intercourse. With the second wife, Ambālikā, he engenders Pāṇḍu, who is as pale as death for, alerted to the mishap of her sister, the young woman had kept her eyes open at the fateful moment, but could not prevent herself turning white with fear. Vyāsa did not stop there, but engendered with a serving woman a third child, who became the wise Vidura.

On the death of Śāntanu, the kingdom is initially bequeathed to Pāṇḍu, the second son, because it is considered a bad omen for the kingdom to be ruled by a blind king. A short time after his coronation, Pāṇḍu marries Kuntī, the future aunt of Kṛṣṇa, who belongs to a distant branch of the family, and the beautiful Mādrī, the daughter of the king of Madra. Unfortunately, he becomes the victim of a curse which condemns him to die the moment he has sexual relations with a woman. So Kuntī reveals a secret to him: she has a *mantra*, a sacred formula, which permits her to have children with any god that she invokes. Pāṇḍu agrees to this compromise on condition that it is he who will choose the gods who beget his descendants himself. Thanks to these supernatural means, and under the orders of her husband, Kuntī first of all gives birth to Yudhiṣṭhira, born of the god Dharma (the Law), then to Bhīma, born of the god Vāyu (the Wind), and finally to Arjuna, born of the god Indra (the Rain, Thunder, and King of the gods). Then she transmits the *mantra* to her co-wife, who becomes in her turn the mother of Nakula and Sahadeva, the twin boys of the Aśvin gods (the Horsemen, twin gods who are divine keepers of the wealth of the gods and their physicians). These five brothers make up the Pāṇḍava clan who will stay united to the end. But what no one knows apart from Kuntī, is that she has already had, before her marriage, a son with the god Sūrya (the Sun). However, she abandoned him, and he was adopted by a married couple of the charioteer caste who named him Karṇa.

For his part, the blind Dhṛtarāṣṭra marries Gāndhārī, who takes a vow to live her entire life with a blindfold round her eyes in order to be equal to her husband. A little later on, Gāndhārī gives birth, very painfully, to a hundred sons who are born in one go from a ball of iron which she carried for two years in her womb. The eldest is Duryodhana, who at the head of his ninety-nine brothers becomes the leader of the Kaurava clan who are opposed to the Pāṇḍava.

In spite of the curse he lives under, Pāṇḍu ends in succumbing to the charms of Mādrī and dies making love to her. Weeping uncontrollably, the young woman throws herself on the king's funeral pyre, and Kuntī adopts her two children. The kingdom is conferred on Dhṛtarāṣṭra, in spite of his handicap. During his regency, the one hundred and five cousins of the two branches of the family are brought up together at the court under the direction of a master of arms, the Brahmin Droṇa.

Once the young men become adults, Dhṛtarāṣṭra is consulted to find out who will inherit the throne. The blind old man, against all expectations, choses as crown prince not his eldest son, Duryodhana, but his nephew, Yudhiṣṭhira, who has a reputation for being a very righteous man. From then on, the ambitious Duryodhana will not cease until he has snatched away the throne that he believes to have been unjustly given to his cousin. In order to avoid an imminent conflict, it is provisionally decided to divide the kingdom in two. The town of Hāstinapura, on the Ganges, remains the capital of Dhṛtarāṣṭra and his sons, while Yudhiṣṭhira and his brothers are installed at Indraprastha, on the Yamunā.

Meanwhile, Drupada, the king of Kāśi (Bénarès), organises a tournament whose prize will be his daughter, Draupadī. All the princes attend, and it is Arjuna who wins. On returning home he calls out to his mother that he has won a contest. But Kuntī, who does not know that the prize is a woman, immediately tells him, 'share the prize with your brothers.' As she cannot go back on her words, Draupadī becomes, thanks to the strength of this oracle, the common wife of the Pāṇḍava. This polyandrous marriage is a happy one, even when later Bhīma and Arjuna have other wives.

After several unsuccessful attempts to eliminate his cousins, Duryodhana invites Yudhiṣṭhira, whose weak spot he knows full well, to a dice game in the course of which he gets his uncle, Śakuni, a notorious cheat, to play in his place. Driven on by his passion for dice, the unfortunate Yudhiṣṭhira begins by losing all his wealth, then his army and his kingdom. He then bets and loses successively his four brothers, himself and then their common wife, Draupadī. Eager to revel in his total victory, Duryodhana asks his brother, Duḥśāsana to go and fetch the young woman and strip her in front of everyone in order to humiliate his cousins. But the wretched young woman, pulled by the hair into the middle of the shocked assembly, has the presence of mind to invoke the name of Kṛṣṇa, a distant cousin of the family who reigns in a neighbouring kingdom. This cousin who is physically absent from these events is said to be an avatar—an earthly incarnation of Viṣṇu, the Supreme divinity. This identity is only sensed by some people and remains unknown to others. By the power of his *māyā*, his power of illusion, Kṛṣṇa produces a miracle. He makes Draupadī's saree become endless in length as Duḥśāsana tries to pull it off, thus ridiculing her tormentors. The wife of the Pāṇḍava then points out that the game of dice was actually technically flawed: Yudhiṣṭhira had bet her when he had already lost himself! He therefore had no right to dispose of her. She thus gains from Dhṛtarāṣṭra, by way of compensation, the release of her five husbands. But they must go into exile for twelve years and stay incognito during the thirteenth before they are allowed to return.

After this long period of waiting and in spite of all Duryodhana's attempts to flush out his cousins in order to destroy them, the Pāṇḍava are able to return to Indraprastha. But this situation cannot satisfy the insatiable Duryodhana. War threatens, in spite of Kṛṣṇa's attempts at reconciliation, when the two clans bring him in to arbitrate between them. Finally the avatar offers the two opponents a choice: one of them can have his personal help, though without him joining in combat, and the other will then have his army without him. The decision falls to Arjuna, who opts for the first choice, and Kṛṣṇa's army is sent over to Duryodhana, who is overjoyed with the deal.

The war is now inevitable and lasts for eighteen days. In the midst of the intense fighting Kṛṣṇa exhorts and advises the Pāṇḍava, not without using some ruses and tricks which the soldiers find morally troubling. But these transgressions are perpetrated only because of the deceit of their enemies, especially Duryodhana. Thus fall one after another the generals and chiefs of the Kaurava army, that is Bhīṣma, Droṇa, Karṇa, and then Śalya. Duryodhana succumbs in single combat against Bhīma. The Pāṇḍava finally win but at a terrible price. What is worse is that Droṇa's son, Aśvatthāman, one of the three remaining survivors of the Kaurava, manages to find a way to massacre the survivors of the Pāṇḍava army in their sleep, including the five sons of Draupadī. The only ones to escape his vengeance are the five brothers and two other soldiers. Aśvatthāman, wishing to complete his work of destruction, targets Arjuna's unborn grandchild, Parikṣit, the last hope of the dynasty, who is still in the womb of his mother Uttarā. But Kṛṣṇa succeeds in stopping him before returning home to Dvārakā. Yudhiṣṭhira can now reign unchallenged over the kingdom of Bhārata. Thirty six years later, having now grown old, he leaves the throne to Parikṣit, Arjuna's grandchild, and retires to the Himalaya with his wife and four brothers who all die on the way. Eventually, after a final trial during which he refuses to give up the dog who accompanies him, and who is none other, in this modest guise, than a manifestation of his father Dharma—which he does not actually realise—he ascends to the heaven of Indra in his body. It is there that he finds his family, in an infernal region from where they are destined to be purified of their last sins before their glorious assumption. Parikṣit now reigns unchallenged over the kingdom of Bhārata and is reputed to be the mythical ancestor of all present day Indians.

Glossary of Main Characters and Sanskrit Terms

Abhimanyu: the Proud, the Enthusiastic. Son of Arjuna and Subhadrā, he died heroically during the war at the age of 16, leaving his wife Uttarā pregnant. He is the incarnation of Soma.

adharma: chaos, confusion. *Adharma* is the opposite of *dharma*.

adharmika: related to *adharma*.

Adhiratha: the Charioteer. With his wife Rādhā, he adopts Karṇa, abandoned by his mother in a basket cast on the waters of a tributary of the Yamunā.

Adhokṣaja: one of the names of Viṣṇu meaning 'He who holds the disc in his lower (left) hand.' Attributed to Kṛṣṇa it means 'He who is born (again) in his cradle.'

ādivāsī: indigenous person. This is the name given to the first inhabitants of India before any invasion or migration. They now account for about 8 per cent of the country's population and are not Hindus.

Agni: Fire.

ahaṃ brahmāsmi: 'I am *brahman*' (*Bṛhadāraṇyakopaniṣad*, 1, 4, 10), a sacred formula considered a *mahāvākya*.

akṣa: wheel; discus.

Ambālikā: diminutive of mother. Second wife of the son of Śāntanu and Satyavatī. She conceived Pāṇḍu with Vyāsa.

Ambikā: diminutive of mother. First wife of the son of Śāntanu and Satyavatī. She conceived Dhṛtarāṣṭra with Vyāsa.

anabhiṣaṅga: non-attachment, renunciation.

Ananta: Infinity. Name of the serpent Śeṣa.

Arjuna: the Brilliant, the Silver One. Son of Kuntī and the god Indra, he is the third Pāṇḍava.

artha: material well-being, wealth, health.

asakti: non-attachment, renunciation.

asura: demon.

Aśvatthāman: Strong as a horse. Name of Droṇa's son. He is the incarnation of Rudra, a terrible form of Śiva.

Aśvin: the Horsemen. Twin gods, bringers of wealth, who perform the role of doctors to the gods.

Ātma-bhū: 'He who is born of Himself.' A name of Brahmā.

ātman: reflexive pronoun. The divine Self or the individual self.

avatāra: descent; incarnation.

ayamātmā brahma: 'This *ātman* is *brahman*, this self is the Absolute' (*Māṇḍūkyopaniṣad*, 2), a sacred formula considered a *mahāvākya*.

Balarāma: Rāma the Powerful. Elder brother of Kṛṣṇa, he shares with him the rank of eighth avatar of Viṣṇu or, more precisely, he embodies Śeṣa, the serpent on which Viṣṇu reclines. He remains neutral in the Kurukṣetra war.

Bhaumāsura: the Demon born of the earth. Name of a demon who held sixteen thousand women prisoners. Kṛṣṇa saved them and made them his wives.

Bhagavat: the Fortunate, the Prosperous, the Adorable, the Lord. Name of Kṛṣṇa. The *Bhagavad-gītā* is, literally, the Song of the Lord.

bhakti: sharing; love, devotion.

bhakti-yoga: path of love or devotion.

Bhārata: name of the descendants of Bharata, the eponymous ancestor of the Indians.

bhava: state, birth.

bhāva: being, existence.

Bhaya: Fear personified.

Bhīma: the Terrible. Son of Kuntī and the god Vāyu, he is the second of the Pāṇḍava.

Bhīṣma: the Terrible. Son of Śāntanu and Gaṅgā, he received this name because of the terrible nature of his double vow to relinquish power and women. He remains faithful to the Kaurava clan despite his affection for the Pāṇḍava.

bhoktṛ: enjoyer.

bhūr-bhuvaḥ svaḥ: 'Earth, Atmosphere (intermediate world), Heaven'. Famous invocation repeated in many Vedic rites.

Brahmā: the Creator. First god of the Hindu *trimūrti*.

brahman: sacred utterance; absolute, infinite. This term in the neuter gender refers to the supreme Reality.

brāhmaṇa: Brahmin, priest; member of the highest caste.

brahmāstra: a missile of Brahmā. A powerful legendary weapon that can burn up the world.

Bṛhaspati: the priest of the gods.

Buddha: the Awakened One; Gautama Buddha, the historical Buddha, regarded by Hindus as an *avatāra* of Viṣṇu.

cakra: discus. Kṛṣṇa's circular weapon.

Candra: the Ash, the Moon god (masculine gender). Ancestor of the lunar dynasty.

Dakṣa: Skill, ritual Art personified.

Damayantī: the Seductive One. Princess and lover of Nala, whose story is incidentally told in the *Mahābhārata*.

Dāmodara: 'He who has a rope around the belly.' Name given to Kṛṣṇa as a child, when his adoptive mother, Yaśodā, wanted to tie him up to prevent him from stealing butter.

darśana: vision, perspective; philosophical school.

dāsya: slavery.

deva: celestial being, god, angel.

Devakī: the Divine, the Dice Player. Name of Kṛṣṇa's mother.

Devī: the Goddess. Generic name of the deity conceived as female, worshipped in the Śaktik and Tantric sects.

dharma: order, law, justice, honour. This term is the etymological equivalent of the Latin *firmus*, firm.

Dharma: the cosmic order personified.

dharmika: according to *dharma*.

Dhṛṣṭadyumna: the Dazzling One. Putative son of King Drupada, he arose from the sacrificial fire at the same time as his twin sister Draupadī. He incarnates Agni and is the commander-in-chief of the Pāṇḍava army.

Dhṛtarāṣṭra: 'He who has a strong empire.' Son of Vyāsa and Ambikā. A blind king, married to Gāndhāri, he is the leader of the Kaurava but is under the control of his son Duryodhana.

Dhṛti: Constance personified.

Dīnabandhu: Friend (or Relative) of the afflicted. A name of Kṛṣṇa.

Draupadī: the daughter of King Drupada (the Pillar of Wood). She was born of the sacrificial fire at the same time as her twin brother, Dhṛṣṭadyumna, and incarnates the Earth.

Droṇa: the Wooden Container. Name of the Brahmin guru of the young Pāṇḍava and Kaurava. He fights on the latter's side and is the father of Aśvatthāman. He is the embodiment of Bṛhaspati, the priest of the gods.

Duḥśāsana: the Evil Councillor. Name of the second of Dhṛtarāṣṭra's hundred sons, who is the evil genius of his elder brother Duryodhana.

Durukti: the Lie personified.

Durvāsas: the Badly Dressed One. Name of the Brahmin welcomed by Kuntī in her youth, who transmitted a *mantra* to her. He is an incarnation of Śiva.

Duryodhana: the One Hard to Fight. Name of the eldest son of Gāndhārī and Dhṛtarāṣṭra, and the real leader of the Kaurava.

dvāpara-yuga: the age designated by the number two. The third Age of the *mahāyuga*, equivalent to the Bronze Age.

Dvārakā: the City of the Gate, Kṛṣṇa's capital, located in Gujarat, on the western tip of India (currently Dwarka).

dvija: twice-born, initiated member of one of the first three castes (*brāhmaṇa*, *kṣatriya*, *vaiśya*).

Dyu: Heaven personified.

Gadādhara: the Mace Bearer. A name of Kṛṣṇa.

Gāndhārī: the Afghan, the woman who comes from Gandhāra. Name of Dhṛtarāṣṭra's wife and mother of the Kaurava.

Gaṅgā: the Fluid One. Name of the goddess of the Gaṅgā, Śāntanu's lover and mother of Bhīṣma.

gītā: song, poem.

gopī: gopi, milkmaid, female cowherd.

Govinda: 'He who finds (or guards) cows.' Name of Kṛṣṇa.

guṇa: bowstring; fundamental quality of nature.

guru: heavy, weighty; venerable, respectable; spiritual master.

haṃsa: swan; symbol of *brahman*, spirit. One of the twelve *mahāvākya* (*Haṃsopaniṣad*, 2–4).

Hanumān: 'He who has jaws.' Name of the general of the army of monkeys, who came to the help of Rāma in the *Rāmāyaṇa* epic. He represents the perfect devotee.

Hara: 'He who takes away'. A name of Śiva.

Hari: the Yellow One, the Fawn-coloured One. Name of Kṛṣṇa.

Hāstinapura: City of the Elephant. Name of the Bhārata capital situated on the Ganges.

Hiḍimba: (uncertain etymology). Name of a demon whose sister falls in love with Bhīma, with whom she has a son.

Hiṃsā: Violence personified.

Hṛṣīkeśa: Master of the Senses (or 'He whose hair stands on end for joy'). Name of Kṛṣṇa.

Indra: the Drop of water. Name of the king of the gods, lord of the rain and thunder.

Indraprastha: seat of Indra. Name of the capital of the Pāṇḍava, near modern Delhi.

iṣṭa-devatā: chosen deity.

īśvara: powerful; Lord, God.

itihāsa: 'he spoke thus'; generic name for the Indian epics.

Jagadguru: Master of the World. Name of Kṛṣṇa and title of the spiritual descendants of Śaṅkara.

jagat: world.

japa: invocation.

Jara: the Old One. Name of the hunter who accidentally kills Kṛṣṇa.

jāti: birth; caste in the socio-professional sense. There are between three and five thousand *jāti* in India.

jīva: living being, individual being.

jīvanmukta: a living fully liberated being.

jñāna: knowledge.

jñānin: knower; one who follows the path of knowledge.

kaivalya: monist; one who sees God as one (*kevala*).

kali: the number one, which represents the worst throw of the dice.

Kālī: the Black One. Name of Devī; another name of Satyavatī.

Kāla: Time personified.

Kāliya: the Black One. Name of a serpent which haunted the Yamunā and that Kṛṣṇa tamed in his childhood.

kali-yuga: the age of the worst throw of the dice; the age of conflicts. The Fourth Age of the *mahāyuga*, equivalent to the Iron Age.

Kalki: the Dirty One. Name of the last *avatāra* of Viṣṇu, who must appear at the end of the present *mahāyuga*. He is depicted as a horseman brandishing a sword or as a man with a horse's head.

kalpa: immense time period equivalent to one day of Brahmā or 14 *manvantara*.

kāma: love, affection.

Kaṃsa: the (metal) Cup. Name of a treacherous king of Mathurā who imprisoned his father Ugrasena. He did everything he could to prevent the birth of Kṛṣṇa, who escaped from him and eventually killed him.

karman: act, sacrificial act.

karma-yoga: sacrificial way, way of works.

Karṇa: the Ear. Eldest son of Kuntī and Sūrya (the Sun). He got his name from the fact that he was born with a breastplate and gold earrings.

Kaurava: descendants of Kuru. Although the Pāṇḍava are also descendants of Kuru, in the *Mahābhārata* the word only means the sons of Dhṛtarāṣṭra and their allies.

kevala: one.

ko'ham: 'Who am I?' Key formula of yoga of questioning (*vicāra-yoga*), as taught by Ramaṇa Maharṣi.

Krodha: Wrath personified.

Kṛṣṇa: the Blue-black. Kṛṣṇa is the eighth major incarnation of Viṣṇu. Arjuna is also sometimes referred to by this name.

Kṛṣṇā: feminine form of the preceding word. Name of Draupadī.

Kṛṣṇa Dvaipāyana: 'the island-born Kṛṣṇa'. Name of Vyāsa.

kṛta-yuga: the Perfect Age. First Age of the *mahāyuga*, the equivalent of the Golden Age.

kṣatriya: man of the (battle) field, warrior; member of the second caste.

kṣetra: battlefield; the world as an object of knowledge.

kuṇḍalinī: the Coiled One; *śakti* of Śiva, wound at the bottom of the spine like a snake.

Kuntī: 'the Woman of the people of Kunti'. Sister of Vāsudeva, Kṛṣṇa's aunt, adopted daughter of Kuntibhoja, wife of Pāṇḍu, mother of the Pāṇḍava and Karṇa.

Kuntibhoja: 'Joy of the Kunti'. Name of the king of the Kunti people, in present day Gujarat, and adoptive father of Kuntī.

Kuru: eponymous ancestor of the Kaurava.

Kurukṣetra: the Field of the Kuru. Site of the battle in the *Mahābhārata*, located on the plains between the Ganges and Yamunā.

Lakṣmī: the Fortunate. Wife of Viṣṇu.

Lalitā: the Lover, the Voluptuous One. Name of Devī. Name of a friend of Rādhā.

Madana: 'He who rejoices', the Intoxicated One. Name of Kāma, the god of love.

Madhu: the Sweet One, Honey. Name of Kṛṣṇa.

Mādrī: 'the Woman of the people of Madra'. Pāṇḍu's second wife and mother of Nakula and Sahadeva.

mahātman: great soul, wise.

mahāvākya: a great saying. Generic word for twelve formulas expressing the supreme identity of *ātman* and *brahman* in the *Upaniṣad*.

mahāyuga: cycle of four ages.

manas: internal sense, mental faculty.

Manu: the Intelligent, the Man. Father of the human race, comparable to Adam. Every *manvantara* is inaugurated by the appearance of a new Manu.

manvantara: era of Manu. An era of Manu, or *manvantara*, contains 71 cycles of the four ages (or *mahāyuga*), which are equivalent to the Golden, Silver, Bronze and Iron Ages of the Greek tradition.

mārga: path, track followed by a hunter, spiritual path. Synonymous with *yoga*.

Mathurā: (uncertain meaning). Name of the city where Kṛṣṇa was born in the kingdom usurped by Kaṃsa. Mathurā is located on the Yamunā, downstream of Delhi.

māyā: measurement; magic, power of illusion.

mokṣa: deliverance.

Mṛtyu: Death personified.

muni: sage, ascetic hermit.

Nakula: the Mongoose. Son of Mādrī and the Aśvin gods. Twin brother of Sahadeva and the fourth Pāṇḍava.

Nala: the Reed. King of Niṣadha and Damayantī's lover.

nāma-rūpa: name and form.

Nanda: Joy, Happiness. Name of the adoptive father of Kṛṣṇa.

Nara: the Man. Name of an ancient *ṛṣi* whose association with Nārāyaṇa prefigures that of Arjuna and Kṛṣṇa.

Nārada: 'He who teaches men.' Name of a divine *ṛṣi*, poet and messenger between men and gods.

Narasiṃha: the Man-lion. Name of the fourth major *avatāra* of Viṣṇu.

Nārāyaṇa: Name of Viṣṇu whose hermeneutical significance is: 'He who is a way for men,' or 'He who is reclining on the waters' (the cosmic ocean).

naṭa: dance, mime.

Naṭarājan: Lord of the Dance. Name of Śiva.

nirukta: said, pronounced; lexicology, hermeneutic interpretation.

niṣkāma-karman: selfless action.

Pāṇḍava: descendants of Pāṇḍu.

Pāṇḍu: the Pale One. Son of Vyāsa and Ambālikā. Husband of Kuntī and Mādrī, putative father of the Pāṇḍava.

paṅka: mud.

paṅkaja: lotus.

parama-haṃsa: supreme swan.

parāyaṇa: refuge; principle.

Parikṣit: 'He who remains, surrounds'. Name of the grandson of Arjuna and Subhadrā. Foremost heir of the Pāṇḍava.

Prabhāsa: the Shining One. Name of a city in Gujarat.

Prabhu: the Mighty, the Rich, the Bountiful. Name of Kṛṣṇa.

Prahlāda: Joy, Pleasure. Name of a king martyred in childhood and saved by Narasiṃha.

prakṛti: nature, feminine principle of manifestation (as opposed to *puruṣa*).

pralaya: dissolution.

Pṛśni: the Spotted One, the Little One. Wife of Sutapas. Name of a queen regarded as a previous incarnation of Devakī.

Pṛthā: the Flat One. Proper name of Kuntī.

Pṛthivī: the Vast Expanse. Name of the goddess Earth.

pūjā: worship, ritual worship.

Puṇyaśloka: 'He of whom good is spoken.' Name of Yudhiṣṭhira.

Pūru: the Abundant One. Son of Yayāti, ancestor of the Paurava.

puruṣa: man; male principle of manifestation (as opposed to *prakṛti*).

Puruṣa: the Principial Man whose self-sacrifice and dismemberment creates the world according to Vedic doctrine.

Pūtanā: the Infernal One (?). Demon sent by Kaṃsa to kill Kṛṣṇa with poisoned milk when he was a baby.

Rādhā: Prosperity, Success. Name of Kṛṣṇa's favourite lover in the *Gīta-Govinda*, by Jayadeva (12th century).

Rādhā: Adhiratha's wife and foster mother of Karṇa.

rajas: colourful (dust, vapour); quality of nature, *guṇa*.

rājasika: rajasic, related to *rajas*.

Rāma: the Pleasant One, the Charming One (etymologically, the Black One). Name of three successive *avatāra* of Viṣṇu: Paraśurāma (Rāma with an axe), Rāmacandra (Rāma, the lunar hero of the *Rāmāyaṇa*), and Balarāma, the elder brother of Kṛṣṇa.

Rāmacandra: the Lunar Rāma, hero of the *Rāmāyaṇa*.

rasa: flavour.

Rohinī: the Red Cow. Second wife of Vāsudeva and mother of Balarāma.

ṛṣi: seer; poet, prophet.

Rudra: the Howler. Name of Śiva.

Rukmiṇī: the Shining One, the One Trimmed with Gold. Wife of Kṛṣṇa.

sādhaka: he who practices *sādhanā*.

sādhanā: worship, spiritual path.

Sahadeva: With the gods. Son of Mādrī and the Aśvin gods. Twin brother of Nakula and the fifth Pāṇḍava.

Śākalya: the Fragmented One (?). Disciple of Yājñavalkya, mentioned in the *Bṛhadāraṇyakopaniṣad*.

śakti: energy, power.

Śakuni: the Bird (of Doom). Brother of Gāndhārī and uncle of the Kaurava. He embodies the *dvāpara-yuga*.

Śakuntalā: the Bird of Prey. Princess of the lunar dynasty and mother of Bharata, eponymous ancestor of the Bhārata.

samādhi: ecstasy (or rather 'enstasy').

saṃkalpa: desire.

Sāṃkhya: enumeration. Name of one of the six *darśana*, or perspectives, of Indian philosophy.

saṃnyāsa: renunciation.

saṃnyāsin: ascetic, hermit.

saṃsāra: flux (of existence), the world.

sanātana-dharma: perennial order, (Hindu) tradition.

Śāntanu: the Handsome One. King of the Kuru, first the lover of Gaṅgā, he begets Bhīṣma with her. Then, as Satyavatī's husband, he begets two sons who die young and childless.

Sarasvatī: 'She who abounds in water.' Name of a mythical river, variously located. Name of the wife of Brahmā.

satī: a woman who throws herself on the funeral pyre of her husband.

sattva: conforming to being, good; quality of nature, *guṇa*.

sāttvika: satvic, related to *sattva*.

Satyabhāmā: 'She who has a lovely radiance.' Wife of Kṛṣṇa.

Satyavatī: the Truthful One. Daughter of the King of the Fish. Mother of Vyāsa, from a union in her youth with a Brahmin. Then wife of Śāntanu, to whom she gives two sons who die young and childless.

Śeṣa: the Remainder. Name of cosmic serpent upon which Viṣṇu Nārāyaṇa reclines; incarnated as Balarāma.

sevana: service, devotion.

Siddhi: Realization personified.

Śiśupāla: Protector of Children (or followers). Cousin full of hatred for Kṛṣṇa. The avatar kills him with his discus after tolerating 99 insults from him.

Sītā: the Furrow. Wife of Rāmacandra and incarnation of Lakṣmī.

Śiva: the Propitious One. Third god of the *trimūrti*.

śloka: verse, stanza.

smaraṇa: remembrance.

smṛti: memory; category of traditional writings.

so'ham: 'I am that' (*Haṃsopaniṣad*, 2–4), formula considered a *mahāvākya*.

soma: strong drink, nectar; Vedic god.

śravaṇa: listening, audition.

śruti: audition; class of traditional writings.

Subhadrā: the Glorious One, the Auspicious One. Sister of Kṛṣṇa; Arjuna's wife; mother of Abhimanyu. She embodies *yoga-nidrā*, the sleep of *yoga*.

śūdra: servant, member of the fourth caste.

sura: celestial being.

Śūra: the Brave One, the Heroic One. Father of Kuntī.

Surāṣṭra: Surat, city of Gujarat.

Sūrya: the Sun. Father of Karṇa.

Sutapas: 'He who practices great asceticism.' Husband of Pṛśni. Name of a king considered a previous incarnation of Vasudeva.

sūtra: wire, suture; generic name of traditional treatises.

tamas: dark, quality of nature, *guṇa*.

tāmasika: tamasic, referring to *tamas*.

tattvamasi: 'Thou art That' (*Chāndogyopaniṣad*, 6, 8, 7), formula considered a *mahāvākya*.

trimūrti: triple manifestation.

tyad: that.

Uddhava: the Sacrificial Fire. Friend and adviser of Kṛṣṇa.

Ugrasena: 'He who has a terrible army.' Unfortunate king of Mathurā, imprisoned by his son Kaṃsa. Uncle of Devakī.

Uttarā: the Best One. Wife of Abhimanyu, mother of Parikṣit.

vaiśya: peasant, herder, artisan, merchant, member of the third caste.

Vasudeva: the Bright Celestial Being. Husband of Devakī and father of Kṛṣṇa.

Vāsudeva: Son of Vasudeva. Name of Kṛṣṇa.

Vāyu: the Wind. Father of Bhīma.

Vedānta: the end of the *Veda* (= *Upaniṣad*); name of one of the six *darśana* or perspectives of Indian philosophy.

Veṅkiteśvara: the Lord of the Veṅkita hill (in Andhra Pradesh). Name of Viṣṇu.

Vibhu: the Omnipresent. Name of Kṛṣṇa.

vicāra-yoga: *yoga* of questioning.

viḍambana: trickery, enigma.

Vidura: the Intelligent One, the Skilful One. Third son of Vyāsa. Half-brother of Dhṛtarāṣṭra and Pāṇḍu. Incarnation of Dharma.

Viṣṇu: the Penetrating One. Second god of the *trimūrti*.

viśva: totality, universe.

Viśvā: Totality. Vedic goddess, mother of the Viśve-deva.

Viśvātman: the Soul of the Universe, the Self of the Universe. Name of Kṛṣṇa.

Viśve-deva: All the gods. Category of Vedic gods.

Viśveśa: the Lord of the Universe. Name of Kṛṣṇa.

Viśvamūrti: the Form of the Universe, the Manifestation of the Universe. Name of Kṛṣṇa.

Viśvarūpa: synonym of the previous.

Vivasvat: the Brilliant One. Name of the Sun.

Vṛndāvana: the Great Forest. Forest where Kṛṣṇa lived in his youth, near Mathurā.

Vṛṣṇi: the Powerful One, the Mighty One. Name of the eponymous king of the Vṛṣṇi, the descendants of Yādava.

Vṛtra: the Enfolder. Mythical serpent or dragon killed by Indra.

Vyāsa: the Diffuser, the Compiler. The title of Kṛṣṇa Dvaipāyana, the author of the *Mahābhārata*.

Yādava: descendant of Yadu. Name of a people and name of Kṛṣṇa.

Yadu (uncertain meaning): ancestor of the Yādava, non-reigning branch of the lunar dynasty.

yajña: sacrifice.

Yājñavalkya: Master of the Sacrifice. Ancient sage mentioned in the *Bṛhadāraṇyakopaniṣad*.

Yamunā: sister of Yama, the god of death. Tributary of the Ganges, now the Jumnā.

Yaśodā: 'She that gives glory.' Wife of Nanda, foster mother of Kṛṣṇa.

Yayāti: 'He who walks straight' (?). King of the lunar dynasty, father of Yadu and Pūru.

yoga: yoke; union; spiritual path.

yoga-nidrā: the sleep of *yoga* (the sleep in question is that of the mind calmed by the *yoga*). Incarnated by Subhadrā.

yogin: *yoga* adept.

Yudhiṣṭhira: 'He who is strong in combat.' Son of Kuntī and the god Dharma. Oldest brother of the Pāṇḍava.

yuga: age, cyclic period.

Bibliography

Abū Bakr Sirāj al-Dīn, *The Book of Certainty*, Samuel Weiser, New York, 1974.

Angot, Michel, *L'Inde classique*, Les Belles Lettres, Paris, 2001.

Banerji, Sures Chandra, *A Companion to Sanskrit Literature*, Motilal Banarsidass, Delhi, 1989.

Bhāgavata-purāṇa: see Prabbhupāda, Tapasyananda.

Biardeau, Madeleine, *Le Mahābhārata, Un récit fondateur du brahmanisme et son interprétation*, éditions du Seuil, Paris, 2002, 2 vols.

Brunner, Fernand, *Science et réalité*, Aubier, éditions Montaigne, 1954.

Buck, William, *Mahabharata*, Motilal Banarsidass, 2000.

Burckhardt, Titus, *Mirror of the Intellect, Essays on Traditional Science and Sacred Art*, Quinta Essentia, Cambridge, 1987.

Chidbhavananda, Swami, *The Bhagavad Gita*, Sri Ramakrishna Tapovanam, Tiruchirappalli, 1969.

Coomaraswamy, Ananda K., *Hinduism and Buddhism*, Greenwood Press, Westport, Connecticut, 1971.

Coomaraswamy, Ananda K., *The Dance of Shiva, Essays on Indian Art and Culture*, Dover Publications, New York, 1985.

Coomaraswamy, Ananda K., 'The Vedānta and Western Tradition', in: *Selected Papers 2, Metaphysics*, edited by Roger Lipsey, Princeton University Press, New Jersey, 1977.

Daniélou, Alain, *The Myths and Gods of India: The Classic Work of Hindu Polytheism*, Bollingen Paperbacks, Princeton, 1991.

Danner, Victor, *Ibn 'Ata' Illah, The Book of Wisdom*, SPCK, London, 1979.

Dumézil, Georges, *Mythe et épopée, l'idéologie des trois fonctions dans les épopées des peuples indo-européens*, vol. 1, Gallimard, Paris, [1968] 1986[5].

Dutt, Romesh C., *Mahabharata, the Epic of Ancient India, condensed into English Verse*, Kindle edition 2012.

Esnoul, Anne-Marie: cf. Sāṃkhya.

Feuerstein, Georg, *Tantra: The Path of Ecstasy*, Shambala Publications, Boston, 1998.

Ganguli, Kisari Mohan, and Neteesh Gupta, *Mahabharata of Krishna-Dwaipayana Vyasa (Complete)*, in 12 vols., or Kindle edition, edited by Darryl Morris, CreateSpace Independent Publishing Platform, 2013.

Geoffroy, Eric, *L'Islam sera spirituel ou ne sera plus*, éditions du Seuil, Paris, 2009.

Georgel, Gaston, *Les quatre Âges de l'humanité*, Archè, Milano, 1976[2].

Gimaret, Daniel, *Les Noms divins en Islam, exégèse lexicographique et théologique*, éditions du Cerf, Paris, 1988.

Gloton, Maurice, *Une Approche du Coran par la grammaire et le lexique*, Albouraq, Beyrouth, 2002.

Guénon, René, *The Great Triad*, translated from the French by Peter Kingsley, Quinta Essentia, Cambridge, 1991.
Guénon, René, *Introduction to the Study of the Hindu Doctrines* (Collected Works of René Guénon), translated from the French by Henry D. Fohr, Sophia Perennis, New York, 2002.
Guénon, René, *Man and His Becoming According to the Vedānta*, translated from the French by R.C Nicholson, Luzac & co., London, 1945.
Guénon, René, *The Reign of Quantity and the Signs of the Times*, translated from the French by Lord Northbourne, Penguin Books Inc., Maryland, 1972.
Guénon, René, *Traditional Forms and Cosmic Cycles* (Collected Works of René Guénon), translated from the French by Henry D. Fohr, Sophia Perennis, New York, 2003.
Harshananda, Swami, *Les Divinités hindoues et leurs demeures*, Dervy-livres, Paris, 1986.
Herbert, Jean, *L'Enseignement de Râmakrishna*, Albin Michel, Paris, [1949] 1972.
Herbert, Jean, *Spiritualité hindoue*, Albin Michel, Paris, [1947] 1972.
Hiltebeitel, Alf, 'Two Kṛṣṇas, Three Kṛṣṇas, Four Kṛṣṇas, More Kṛṣṇas: Dark Interactions in the Mahābhārata', in *Essays on the Mahābhārata*, edited by Arvind Sharma, Motilal Banarsidass, Delhi, 2011, p. 101ff.
Ibn 'Arabī, Muḥyī al-dīn, *The Wisdom of the Prophets (Fuṣūṣ al-Ḥikam)*, translation and notes by Titus Burckhardt, translated from the French by Angela Culme-Seymour, Beshara publications, 1975.
Ibn 'Ata'illah: see Danner, Victor.

Jayadeva, *Love Song of the Dark Lord, Jayadeva's Gīta-Govinda*, edited and translated by Barbara Stoler Miller, Columbia University Press, New York, 1977.

Journet, Charles, *Saint Nicolas de Flue*, éditions Saint-Paul, Fribourg, Paris, 1984.

Koestler, Arthur, *The Sleepwalkers, A History of Man's changing vision of the Universe*, Hutchinson, London, 1959.

Lings, Martin, *Muhammad: His Life based on the Earliest Sources*, Islamic Texts Society, George Allen and Unwin, London, 1983.

Lings, Martin, *Symbol and Archetype: a Study of the Meaning of Existence*, Fons Vitae, Louisville, 2006.

M., *The Gospel of Sri Ramakrishna*, translated from Bengali by Swami Nikhilananda, Ramakrishna-Vivekananda Center, New York, 1942.

Mahābhārata: see Biardeau, Buck, Dutt, Ganguli and Gupta, Menon, Narayan, Smith, and Subramanian.

Menon, Ramesh, *The Mahabharata: A Modern Rendering*, Rupa & co., 2007.

Michaël, Tara, *Yoga*, éditions du Rocher et du Seuil, Paris, 1980.

Michon, Cyrille, *Thomas d'Aquin et la controverse sur l'éternité du monde*, Flammarion, Paris, 2004.

Mookerjee, Ajit, *Tantra Asana, a Way to Self-realisation*, Ravi Kumar, Basel, 1971.

Narayan, R. K., *Mahabharata*, Penguin Modern Classics, London, 2001.

Padoux, André, *Comprendre le tantrisme, les sources hindoues*, Albin Michel, Paris, 2010.

Porte, Alain, *Les dernières Paroles de Krishna, Uddhava Gītā*, traduit du sanskrit par Alain Porte, éditions du Relié et du Seuil, Paris, 1999.

Prabhupāda, A.C. Bhaktivedanta Swami, *The Srimad-Bhagavatam*, Bhaktivedanta Book Trust, 1977, 30 vols.

Prabhupāda, A.C. Bhaktivedanta Swami, *Teachings of Queen Kuntī*, Bhaktivedanta Book Trust, 1990.

Rupa, Gosvami, *The Nectar of Instruction, An Authorized English Presentation of Srila Rupa Gosvami's* Śrī Upadeśamṛta *by A.C. Bhaktivedanta Swami Prabhupada*, Bhaktivedanta Book Trust, 1977.

Sailley, Robert, *Chaitanya et la dévotion à Krishna*, Dervy-livres, Paris, 1986.

Sāṃkhya-kārikā: *Les Strophes de Sāṃkhya, avec le commentaire de Gauḍapāda*, texte sanskrit et traduction annotée par Anne-Marie Esnoul, Les Belles Lettres, Paris, 1964.

Schuon, Frithjof, *Esoterism as Principle and as Way*, translated from the French by William Stoddart, Perennial Books Ltd, Middlesex, 1981.

Schuon, Frithjof, *Light on the Ancient Worlds*, translated from the French by Lord Northbourne, Perennial Books, London, 1965.

Schuon, Frithjof, *Treasures of Buddhism*, World Wisdom, Bloomington, 1993.

Smith, John D., *Mahabharata, an Abridged Translation*, Penguin Books Ltd, London, 2009.

Subramanian, Kamala, *Mahabharata*, Bharatiya Vidya, Bhavan, Bombay, 1982.

Tapasyananda, Swami, *Srimad Bhagavata*, translated by Swami Tapasyananda, Sri Ramakrishna Math, Madras, 1980, 4 vols.

www.ingramcontent.com/pod-product-compliance
Lightning Source LLC
Chambersburg PA
CBHW031956040426
42448CB00006B/384
* 9 7 8 1 9 0 8 0 9 2 1 6 8 *